MASONS
M

Environmental law for the construction industry

Second edition
Masons' guide

Amanda Stubbs

Christopher Dering, Consulting Editor

Thomas Telford

Published by Thomas Telford Publishing, Thomas Telford Ltd, 1 Heron Quay, London E14 4JD. URL: http://www.thomastelford.com

Distributors for Thomas Telford books are
USA: ASCE Press, 1801 Alexander Bell Drive, Reston, VA 20191-4400, USA
Japan: Maruzen Co. Ltd, Book Department, 3-10 Nihonbashi 2-chome, Chuo-ku, Tokyo 103
Australia: DA Books and Journals, 648 Whitehorse Road, Mitcham 3132, Victoria

First edition 1998
Second edition 2002

A catalogue record for this book is available from the British Library

ISBN: 0 7277 3095 9

Throughout this book the personal pronouns 'he', 'his', etc are used when referring to 'the contractor', 'the client', etc. for reasons of readability. Readers should consider these pronouns to be grammatically neuter in gender, rather than masculine, in all cases.

This book is published on the understanding that the author is solely responsible for the statements made and opinions expressed in it and that its publication does not necessarily imply that such statements and/or opinions are or reflect the views or opinions of the publishers. While every effort has been made to ensure that the statements made and the opinions expressed in this publication provide a safe and accurate guide, no liability or responsibility can be accepted in this respect by the author or publishers.

Typeset by Mary O'Hara
Printed and bound in Great Britain by MPG Books, Bodmin

Preface

Environmental law for the construction industry is not written for lawyers. Rather, it is intended to be a practical guide for those working on construction sites who have to deal with environmental law 'at the sharp end'. In this fast-moving area of law, problems can occur very quickly and regulators frequently respond just as fast. It is often not clear who is responsible for environmental issues and for this reason there is a tendency for them to become marginalised until such time as a problem occurs. For this reason this book is aimed primarily at contractors, although it will clearly be relevant to all those within the industry who have some level of responsibility for, or interest in, environmental issues.

This second edition of the Guide, like its predecessor, has been written in broadly chronological order and, to assist with project planning, it should ideally be read from cover to cover. There is a summary in the form of a chronological checklist in Chapter 10. However, it is anticipated that the book will be used mainly as a quick reference manual which can be read selectively when information about a specific topic is required. For this reason every effort has been made to 'signpost' the reader to relevant sections within this book which may have some bearing on the topic in question and, where appropriate, suggestions for further reading (of guidance materials for example) have been made. This second edition offers a number of website addresses as potential sources of further information, acknowledging the internet as a remarkable research tool, among other things. However, its fast moving ever-changing nature means that in months to come the addresses may prove a source of frustration if sites have moved, been re-structured or simply become obsolete. For this one can only apologise, but 'tis the nature of the beast.

This second edition has involved a full revision of all sections previously covered, with a new addition in the form of Chapter 9, which looks at crisis management in the context of environmental matters such as pollution events and protest actions. While attempting to cover a range of environmental issues thought likely to be relevant to the mainstream construction industry, the emphasis has been on producing a user-friendly summary intended to simplify some of the complexity and confusion which surrounds this area of law. It makes no claims to be the 'final word' on the subject — there are already a number of comprehensive textbooks on environmental law in print, as well as legal publications specific to the construction industry. It is hoped that it is easy to follow, with enough information for most situations and indicative of those where further advice should be sought.

The author has endeavoured to state the law as at 31 October 2001.

ACKNOWLEDGEMENTS

Writing a book is a lonely affair when compared with working for clients and being part of a team; interactions with others tend to consist of posing the occasional legal conundrum and requesting help with research and proof-reading. However, the author would like to thank all those friends and colleagues at Masons who responded so whole-heartedly to being badgered throughout production of this book, and in particular Karen Cooksley and her London team, Stephen Chalcraft, Colette McCormack, Jo Hannah and Claire Greenwood in Manchester, and of course, Christopher Dering, without whom the book would have been considerably more rambling and inaccurate. Special thanks also to Dr Richard Kimblin, leading environmental law barrister, for his comments in relation to Chapter 9.

Biographies of the authors

AMANDA STUBBS

Amanda has a masters degree in Environmental Law and has practised in this field since joining Masons in 1990. She advises companies of all types, but the Firm's client base has meant that she has had considerable experience of advising construction companies on procedural and compliance issues relating to environmental law, while having particular experience in land regeneration projects. The Firm's increasing involvement in PFI/PPP projects has provided opportunities to consider a wide range of environmental issues associated with major projects, from advice on waste, contaminated land and groundwater pollution to project risk management and environmental insurance.

She has drafted agreements in respect of waste-to-energy projects, advised on environmental impact assessment and environmental constraints in the context of major development and civil engineering projects; defended companies prosecuted for water pollution and waste management offences; and advised companies bringing civil actions for nuisances such as dust, odours and methane.

She is a member of the UK Environmental Law Association and the CBI Environment Committee for the North West, and has lectured and written extensively on a range of environmental topics.

CHRISTOPHER DERING

Chris joined Masons in 1989, after a period as a lecturer at Exeter College, Oxford, and has been a Partner in the firm since 1992. He moved from the London office to the Hong Kong office in 1998. He practices in the fields of construction, engineering and major projects and has been responsible for the firm's health and safety group.

In terms of construction experience, he has been involved in a wide variety of contentious and non-contentious matters, including in recent times the resolution of disputes arising out of the Channel Tunnel project, North Sea oil platform construction litigation and disputes in relation to major projects in South East Asia and the PRC. He has also advised on land development (including land subject to heavy contamination), rail projects within Hong Kong and elsewhere in the Asia Pacific region and water concession projects in developing countries.

His health and safety experience has mainly been in relation to compliance issues within the construction industry.

Chris has lectured and written on many subjects both publicly and in-house, for government organisations and others.

Chris is a former editor of the *Jersey Law Reports*, a contributor to *Service Level Agreements*, co-editor and co-author of *Eco-Management and Eco-Auditing: Environmental Issues in Business*, consulting editor of the two companion volumes to the present (*Health and Safety Law for the Construction Industry* and *Employment Law for the Construction Industry*) and was a founder member of the editorial board of *Facilities Management Legal Update*.

Abbreviations

APC	Air Pollution Control
CAR	Contractors' All Risks
CHIP Regulations	Chemicals (Hazard Information and Packaging for Supply) Regulations 1994
CICS	Common Incident Classification Scheme
COMAH Regulations	Control of Major Accident Hazards Regulations 1999
COPA 1974	Control of Pollution Act 1974
COSHH Regulations	Control of Substances Hazardous to Health Regulations 1994
CPRE	Council for the Protection of Rural England
D and O	Directors' and Officers' Liability
DoE	Department of the Environment
DETR	Department of the Environment, Transport and the Regions
DTLR	Department of Transport, Local Government and the Regions
EAR	Employers' All Risks
EHO	Environmental Health Officer
EIA	Environmental Impact Assessment
EIL	Environmental Impairment Liability
EL	Employers' Liability
EPA 1990	Environmental Protection Act 1990
HMIP	Her Majesty's Inspectorate of Pollution
HRA 1998	Human Rights Act 1998

ICE	Institution of Civil Engineers
IPC	Integrated Pollution Control
IPPC	Integrated Pollution Prevention and Control
NRA	National Rivers Authority
OFWAT	Office of Water Services
PFI	Private Finance Initiative
PI	Professional Indemnity
PL	Public Liability
PPC	Pollution and Prevention Control
PPE	Personal Protective Equipment
PPG	Planning Policy Guidance Note
PRPs	Potentially Responsible Parties
RSPB	Royal Society for the Protection of Birds
SPC	Special Purpose Company
TCPA 1990	Town and Country Planning Act 1990
WAMITAB	Waste Management Industry Training and Advisory Board
WIA 1991	Water Industry Act 1991
WML	Waste Management Licence
WRA	Waste Regulation Authority
WRA 1991	Water Resources Act 1991

Contents

1

The UK legal framework and the regulators

1.1. INTRODUCTION

This Chapter is intended to provide a brief introduction to the way in which environmental law in the UK is structured, the general legal principles on which it is based, and how and by whom it is enforced.

1.2. BACKGROUND TO ENVIRONMENTAL LAW IN THE UK

Environmental protection and control are not new concepts in the UK. In the last few years, however, the law in this area has developed significantly. There have been fundamental changes in philosophy and direction and increasingly stringent environmental standards have been imposed. This has happened for a variety of reasons, including the development of scientific knowledge, increased public and political awareness of environmental issues, and policy and legislative pressure from the European Union.

UK environmental law is rooted in both statute and the common law. Common-law rights relate primarily to an individual's entitlement to physical well-being, protection of his moveable goods and a right to the use and enjoyment of his land. The role of the

1

common law in environmental protection results primarily from the important role it has played in protecting private interests in land; as a means to address disputes relating to activities on land, through restricting the use of land. It is not, however, a system of law which has been methodically created with the aim of achieving a certain end, but has evolved through a process of judicial law-making, according to precedents established in previous cases. This can lead to the creation of anomalies and inconsistencies. In addition, judges cannot develop areas of law in the way in which they may choose or at a time when such change may appear to be warranted to take account of changing circumstances; they may only determine the law relating to matters which are brought before them.

Where, as a matter of policy, it is felt that certain issues need to be addressed by means of specific law it is for Parliament to introduce changes by way of statute. In the UK there has been a significant increase in the number of specifically environmental statutes because the common law and existing legislation have not been deemed capable of providing a sufficient degree of environmental protection. During the course of the twentieth century many such statutes were brought into force such as

- the Alkali, etc. Works Regulation Act 1906
- the Public Health Act 1936
- the Clean Air Acts of 1956 and 1968, and
- the Health and Safety at Work etc. Act and the Control of Pollution Act, both of 1974.

However, the 1990s was the real decade for environmental change, with major pieces of environmental legislation such as the Environmental Protection Act 1990, the Water Resources Act 1991 and the Environment Act 1995 being enacted.

The principal driving force behind this rapid expansion of the UK's environmental regulatory framework has been membership of the European Union. On account of the European origin of much of the UK's current environmental protection legislation, a basic understanding of the European legal system is helpful.

In other EU countries the legal system is based upon written codes which use relatively broad language, certainly much broader and more general than is the case for statutes in the UK. This means that a good deal of supplementing and interpretation of the written word is required from the courts. Of course, the English courts commonly engage in the interpretation of legislation, but there is an important difference of approach. When assessing legal liabilities in mainland Europe it is necessary to look at the original context in which the codes were drafted, in order to interpret the law. The words of the legislation must be interpreted in a way which achieves the objectives of the original draftsmen of the legislation, which can mean that one ends up with interpretations which are not the same as one would expect from just reading the legislation. This is a different concept from that used in the interpretation of UK legislation but it is the approach which has to be adopted in interpreting EU legislation (regulations, directives and so on), which follows the mainland style in this regard, and, in turn, the UK legislation which implements it.

The European Court of Justice has supreme authority on matters of European law which enables it – if asked – to review the legitimacy of the actions of the other European institutions (the Commission, the Council and the European Parliament), to provide answers on matters of European law to Member States' courts and to declare whether Member States are implementing European law properly. Over the years the European Court of Justice has extended the scope of its powers to the point where an understanding of the Court's view is now central to any discussion of European-based law.

1.3. WHO IS LIABLE AND FOR WHAT?

The general philosophy behind modern environmental legislation is that 'polluters should pay'. However, this does not only mean the person directly responsible for the pollution, but can include owners and occupiers of the land on or from which the pollution emanates, or the directors and senior managers of a business operating on that land. Environmental liability can arise in the context of criminal law, i.e. from statutory controls, and within the framework of civil law, generally based on breaches of contract and the law of tort.

1.3.1. Criminal liability

Criminal liability in the context of environmental law essentially arises out of statutory controls. In criminal law the prosecution must prove beyond reasonable doubt that the defendant is guilty of the offence. However, there is an increasing tendency for environmental legislation in the UK to be underpinned by a *strict* criminal liability regime. Where liability is 'strict', it is not necessary for it to be proven that the defendant intended the particular event or harm to happen or was negligent, but simply that it did happen. Strict liability is therefore 'no-fault' liability. This is in contrast to most criminal offences in which both the defendant's wrongful act and his intention to commit the offence must be proved. However, environmental offences tend to be regarded by the courts as distinct from other criminal acts, as in the words of Wright J. in *Sherras v. De Rutzen*, they 'are not criminal in any real sense, but are acts which in the public interest are prohibited under a penalty'. Environmental offences are therefore often referred to as *'quasi-criminal'* in nature.

Generally speaking, in the first instance it will be the polluter who will be the focus of regulatory attention and court enforcement action. In environmental statutes a polluter is commonly defined as someone who 'causes' or 'knowingly permits' pollution (e.g. s.78F(2) EPA 1990). Causing pollution is a concept which has been subject to interpretation by the courts. It does not require fault or intent to be shown, i.e. it is strict liability. It is satisfied if someone does something which sets off a natural chain of events. In *R v. CPC (UK) Ltd* the court held that a company caused pollution although a spillage was accidental and due to a latent defect in pipework installed for a previous owner. 'Knowingly permitting' pollution has also been subject to interpretation by the courts. It includes situations where a person actually or constructively (where someone ought to know) knows a particular state of affairs exists but does nothing about it although he has the power to do so.

Owners and occupiers of land and premises are very often the focus for environmental liability, both in statute and common law, because, even if they did not create the source of the pollution or cause the polluting event, they are in control of an area which is causing, or has the potential to cause, environmental problems.

By statute, there are generally two circumstances in which liability could attach to the current owner and/or occupier of land

- where the polluter, who is essentially liable for an environmental problem, cannot be identified and/or located (e.g. statutory nuisance under s.80 EPA 1990 or the statutory clean-up regime in respect of contaminated land at ss.78A-78YC EPA 1990)
- where liability attaches to the person who caused or knowingly permitted pollution (e.g. s.161A WRA 1991). While not directly responsible for the polluting matter, an owner or occupier might still be deemed to be *causing* pollution by virtue of the state of his land, or *knowingly permitting* the pollution where he becomes aware that there is an environmental problem about which he does nothing.

The statutory definition of the term 'owner' has been settled for many years as being someone who is entitled to receive the rack-rent of the premises in question (or would be if the premises were let) whether on his own account or as agent or trustee for someone else (e.g. s.343(1) Public Health Act 1936 and s.78A(9) EPA 1990). The term 'rack-rent' has been the subject of a number of attempts at definition but is generally held to mean the full or nearly the full annual market rent for the property. Under these definitions it is not merely the freeholder who is considered the owner of land or premises; tenants can also be owners, and the longer the lease and the greater the tenant's rights under the lease (e.g. to assign or sub-let), the more likely he is to be regarded as an owner.

Liability as an occupier is likely to attach to two classes of person

- tenants
- licensees, potentially including contractors working on the land and/or premises.

Personal liability

Most environmental legislation (e.g. the EPA 1990, WRA 1991 and the Health and Safety at Work etc. Act 1974) contains provisions imposing potential *personal* criminal liability on the directors and senior managers of a company which has been found guilty of an environmental offence. Although the statutory wording needs to be checked in each case, generally in order for individual liability to attach to corporate environmental offences certain pre-conditions must exist.

- The company must be guilty of the offence in question, although the regulatory authority has the discretion whether to prosecute the company and/or the individual responsible. In practice the Environment Agency invariably issues claims against both the company and its directors at the same time. The claim against the directors is then usually dropped in the course of the proceedings because of the difficulty for an external body in the position of the Agency of proving consent or connivance. However, the claim against the directors is viewed by the Agency as a useful tool of negotiation in the early stages of litigation.
- The offence must have been committed with the consent or connivance of, or to have been attributable to, neglect on the part of the individual concerned.

The classes of person who can be held personally liable for a company's offences are its directors, managers, company secretary or similar officers or people who purport to act in such capacities. The test is essentially whether the individual is in a position to control and guide the corporate body in terms of policy and strategy (*Woodhouse v. Walsall MBC*).

An individual who falls within this category is held to consent to the commission of an offence by his company if he is well aware of what is going on and agrees to it, and to connive at an offence where he is well aware of what is going on but his agreement is tacit, resulting not from actively encouraging what happens but letting it continue and saying nothing about it (see *Huckerby v. Elliott*). No absolute duty is imposed on an individual and therefore some act or omission amounting to neglect must be shown if he is to attract liability for neglect resulting in an environmental offence.

Several directors and senior managers have been convicted of 'environmental' offences, although prosecutions of individuals are still more common in the area of health and safety. The penalties involved for environmental offences include fines, community service, remediation requirements and imprisonment.

The Company Directors (Disqualification) Act 1986 gives courts the power to disqualify directors who are convicted of offences in connection with the management of a company for up to 15 years where the case is heard in the Crown Court, and up to five years where it is dealt with by magistrates. Although there have only been a couple of directors disqualified for commission of environmental offences, the powers have been used slightly more in the context of health and safety offences. However, those directors that have been disqualified thus far have operated in small companies where the chain of command is sufficiently transparent to see who was directly responsible for the situation which led to commission of an offence; the consent, connivance or neglect of directors in large corporate structures is likely to be harder to pinpoint.

Criminal sanctions
The penalties for environmental offences include imprisonment (generally up to six months in the Magistrates' Court and up to two years in the Crown Court), fines (up to £20 000 in the Magistrates' Court and unlimited in the Crown Court and sometimes with an additional daily rate until the environmental problem is resolved) and a requirement to remedy the problem.

In certain circumstances a 'Formal Caution' can be an alternative to prosecution where the Environment Agency wishes to deal quickly and simply with offences which it considers to be less serious. Where a Formal Caution is offered but refused, a prosecution will normally be pursued. A Formal Caution is not a form of sentence and cannot be made conditional upon satisfactory completion of a specific task – only the courts may impose such requirements. A Formal Caution is a serious matter which is formally recorded and may influence future decisions to institute proceedings where an offence is repeated. It may be cited in any subsequent court proceedings. A Formal Caution given as a criminal sanction should not be confused with a caution given by an officer prior to asking questions concerning an offence.

The following conditions must be met before a Formal Caution can be administered

- there must be evidence of the offender's guilt sufficient to give a realistic prospect of conviction
- the offender must admit the offence
- the offender must understand the significance of the offence and give informed consent to being cautioned.

Companies should also be aware that insurance is unlikely to provide any assistance in the context of criminal sanctions.

- Where statutory obligations are punishable by way of criminal fines, such fines are rarely recoverable by way of insurance, as a matter of public policy.
- The fact that much environmental legislation is based on the concept of strict liability means that defence costs or clean-up costs are unlikely to be recoverable by way of insurance either, as cover tends only to be available for obligations qualified by the use of 'reasonable skill and care' – it is seldom applicable to absolute obligations, as exist in the world of strict liability.

Therefore criminal fines and related expenses will usually have to be paid directly out of company profits.

1.3.2. Civil liability

Civil liability is featuring increasingly in environmental law. Whereas in criminal law the prosecution must prove beyond reasonable doubt that the defendant is guilty of the offence, the standard of proof in civil cases rests only on the balance of probabilities. Furthermore, it should be noted that the damages which result from civil liability claims are potentially significantly larger than the typical fines imposed in cases of criminal liability. It is important to consider the commercial implications of civil litigation, which can be time-consuming and expensive, both in terms of professional fees and the financial costs associated with delay to projects.

At common law the polluter will be the person who is shown to have inflicted environmental problems on a third party, often by reason of having allowed substances over which the polluter has control to interfere with the third party's rights. As with the statutes, the common law goes further than just looking for a person who, by his positive act, inflicts damage on another. The law will impose responsibilities on people to take steps to protect others where such a duty is warranted for a particular reason; for example, a landowner who uses hazardous substances on his land owes a duty of care to his neighbour to prevent the substances escaping and damaging his neighbour's property (*Halsey v. Esso Petroleum*). As with criminal liability, civil liability can attach to owners and occupiers of land – who may not be 'polluters' as such – simply by reason of their ownership of land which harbours potential environmental problems. The detail of these matters will be considered further below.

1.3.2.1. Liability in contract

A person may agree to take on liability for environmental issues in the context of a particular project or transaction. Such a situation could arise, for example, under

- a contract for works – which might require a contractor to adhere to certain statutory controls, such as health and safety requirements, waste management controls or noise level specifications. Where specified statutory requirements are not complied with, the contractor not only runs the risk of prosecution by a regulatory authority for having committed a criminal offence but he may also be sued for breach of contract, or
- an environmental indemnity where the parties allocate environmental risk and liability between themselves on a property transaction or as part of a corporate acquisition. A party which has the benefit of an indemnity has the advantage that it can claim in respect of any breach without the need to keep its losses as low as possible, as is usually required.

It is wise to give proper regard to any environmental liabilities imposed by contract and to consider whether the risks are allocated fairly according to the relative commercial bargaining positions of the parties, past land-use history, compliance records, known and perceived environmental problems at the site, the attitude of the regulatory authorities to the site and the activities carried out there, and the financial implications associated with any potential liabilities. For a property transaction involving contaminated land, for example, the structuring of contractual environmental liabilities is particularly relevant in the context of the statutory framework for remediation of contaminated land. Under this regime, set out in Part IIa of the EPA 1990 and the accompanying statutory guidance, possible liability exclusion tests hinge on:

- whether the property was sold 'with information', i.e. did the purchaser know what he was buying and was this knowledge reflected in the purchase price?
- whether the contracting parties specified the method in which subsequent remediation would be funded and carried out; if they did, the relevant authority should honour their contractual arangement rather than apportion liability on its own terms.

Hence subsequent apportionment of remediation liability may be determined on the basis of any contractual relationship between the potentially responsible parties. The law in this area is described in more detail in Chapter 4.

1.3.2.2. Liability in tort

A contract claim can in practice only be brought by a party to the contract. Civil actions in relation to environmental issues may also be brought by a third party such as a neighbour whose land is affected by activities on a construction site, or by environmental interest groups trying to prevent or delay a construction project. These third party claims can be broadly classified as tort claims.

The key areas of potential tortious liability to be aware of in the context of environmental law are nuisance, strict liability for foreseeable damage caused by escapes resulting from 'non-natural' uses of land (known as 'the rule in *Rylands v. Fletcher*'), negligence and trespass.

Nuisance

Nuisance occurs when some condition or activity interferes with the use or enjoyment of land. Nuisance is distinguished from the other torts as it seeks to protect proprietary rights as well as restrict an individual's conduct.

Where the nuisance affects the rights of a number of persons it may be classified as a public nuisance. It will be a matter of fact in each case as to whether the number of people affected is great enough to mean that a public as opposed to a private nuisance has been perpetrated. Public nuisance is a crime. Those affected cannot generally bring private actions in respect of a public nuisance unless they have suffered a particular or special loss.

Private nuisance is defined as an unlawful interference by a person with another's use and enjoyment of his land. Not every interference will constitute an actionable nuisance: it must be 'unreasonable', since the law of nuisance seeks to balance the right of the owner of the land to do what he likes on it against the right of owners of neighbouring land to be free from interference.

A recent example of a successful nuisance action involved a demolition contractor who was carrying out works in a property adjacent to premises being used by specialist sound engineers to the film and television industries (*Video London Sound Studios v. Asticus (GMS) and Keltbray Demolition Ltd*). The demolition works caused a relatively small amount of debris and dust to fall from the claimant's chimney into its basement, resulting in damage to sensitive electronic equipment. The cost of repairs exceeded £226 000 and Video London brought a claim in nuisance (among other things) against Keltbray. The judge held that to establish nuisance it is necessary to show conduct which either causes encroachment akin to trespass, causes physical damage to a neighbour's land or buildings, or unduly interferes with the neighbour's comfortable and convenient enjoyment of his land.

Had the consequences of the defendant's operations been limited to interference with the claimant's enjoyment of its property, the claim would probably have failed. However, the judge emphasised that physical damage had been done to the chimney and that this was the true basis of the claim. In these circumstances, the judge concluded, the damage to the equipment was a reasonably foreseeable consequence of the defendant's actions (Keltbray were aware of previous occasions when dust and debris had affected Video London's premises) and the claim succeeded.

However, the right of private action is restricted, so that only those who have suffered direct foreseeable interference with their physical well-being, their personal property or their use or enjoyment of land, can sue. In *Hunter and Others v. Canary Wharf Ltd and London Docklands Development Corporation* the House of Lords stated that only a person with an interest in land could sue in nuisance, i.e. a freehold owner or a tenant of leasehold property, but not family members or casual lodgers, because the action is brought in respect of acts against the landowner's enjoyment of his rights over his land.

The law of statutory nuisance represents a bridge between the private law of nuisance and the more characteristic statutory mechanisms. Like private nuisance it provides protection of the environment indirectly, having developed as a public health mechanism. It is dealt with in more detail in Section 7.3.

The rule in Rylands v. Fletcher

This cause of action is generally said to relate to strict liability for foreseeable damage caused by escapes occasioned by non-natural use of land.

The nineteenth-century case of *Rylands v. Fletcher* concerned a reservoir created by the owner of the land from which water escaped, flooding a mine on neighbouring land. The owner of the reservoir was held to be liable for the damage caused.

The question of what constitutes a non-natural use of land is frequently debated, particularly as many commentators feel that although referred to by one of the Law Lords in the original case, it was not intended that it should become one of the criteria for establishing liability. However, the definition has tended to move with the times and it is doubtful now that a reservoir would be considered a non-natural use.

In a case called *Cambridge Water Company v. Eastern Counties Leather*, the rule in *Rylands v. Fletcher* was discussed in a modern context. In 1980 a new European Directive on drinking water quality effectively heralded a tightening of UK standards. The Water Company found that a borehole from which it abstracted public drinking water no longer complied with the relevant standards, and had to cease using the borehole as a public water supply. It brought an action against Eastern Counties Leather for injunctive relief and damages, on the basis that Eastern Counties had polluted the borehole and therefore a right of ownership had been interfered with. The case finally reached the House of Lords, by which time the only issue was liability under *Rylands v. Fletcher*. The court found that Eastern Counties Leather was not liable to pay damages as the environmental harm had not been reasonably foreseeable. This, of course, leaves open the possibility of a successful action under *Rylands v. Fletcher* if damage caused by an escape is reasonably foreseeable.

Negligence
It is possible for liability in negligence to arise in relation to environmental problems. However, in order to establish such liability, there has to be

- a duty of care owed to the claimant by the defendant
- a breach of that duty, and
- damage caused as a result of the breach.

This is the test to be adopted for claims for damage to property and personal injury. A good example of the application of this test was in the Court of Appeal case, *Hunter and Others v. Canary Wharf Ltd and London Docklands Development Corporation*. A group of local residents successfully brought a claim in negligence for dust arising from nearby construction work. The plaintiffs complained of substantial quantities of dust which had been deposited on their properties during the construction of the 'Limehouse Link Road'. Although it is well established that dust deposits can give rise to an action in nuisance (*Pwllbach Colliery v. Woodman*), the Court of Appeal decided that the deposit of dust on property was 'damage' for the purposes of any right to sue in negligence, and that annoyance and discomfort associated with the deposition of dust and dealing with the dust were capable of founding a claim for damages for negligence. Although the judge was not called upon to fix levels of general damages, in practice these could range from £100 to £1000 for each successful plaintiff, in addition to any actual losses, such as the cost of cleaning curtains and upholstery.

One of the major drawbacks of trying to bring an action in negligence is the fact that it is difficult to recover damages for pure economic loss — as opposed to physical damage to people or property. This is particularly significant in the context of contaminated land where, unless the land undergoes a physical change during the course of ownership, there is less likely to be physical damage. Physical damage can occasionally result from landfill gas explosions or the corrosive or erosive effects of chemicals upon certain types of structure, but the damage suffered by the potential plaintiff is far more likely to be the diminution in commercial value of, for example, property which is found to be built on a seriously contaminated site. Financial blight can arise whether or not there is any actual danger from the contaminants, simply because of the perception that there is an environmental problem which may result in harm or liability in the future.

The question of diminution of value was at the heart of the recent Court of Appeal case, *Blue Circle Industries Plc v. Ministry of Defence*. Damages were awarded in respect of liability under the Nuclear Installations Act 1965, but issues such as the extent of recovery for financial blight will probably be of more general application. The case involved radioactive material from the Atomic Weapons Establishment being washed onto the plaintiff's land during heavy rains. The material contaminated a small area of marshland, necessitating excavation works to clean up the land and these were paid for by the Ministry of Defence. However, when Blue Circle was made aware of the polluting incident it was negotiating to sell the site. Disclosure of the contamination caused the sale to be aborted and Blue Circle brought an action to recover some £5million in damages arising out of diminution of the value of the estate. At first instance the judge stated:

> 'If following repair, the property remains less valuable or less useful, or the plaintiff suffers other financial loss which is consequential on the physical damage, then compensation should be payable in respect of that loss ... provided (those losses) are of a kind which are reasonably foreseeable.'

The view that the damages award should reflect the difference between the plaintiff's position as it would have been without contamination and as it in fact turned out — with a percentage reduction to reflect the uncertainty of the sale — was upheld by the Court of Appeal. Consequential losses were also awarded to reflect losses incurred in running the estate, costs associated with the clean-up including scientific evaluation, legal fees, the regulator's costs and management time. The key to Blue Circle's success in this claim was the fact that the losses flowed from a *physical* change which rendered the property less valuable during the course of their ownership.

If an alleged negligent act results in physical damage to property, a plaintiff's chances of success are much better than for claims involving pure economic loss. The easiest way to bring a claim for straightforward diminution in value is if a contractual basis for the claim exists. In the absence of a contract, it is generally necessary to identify what the courts call a 'special relationship'. A relationship of this kind will, if negligence is proved, mean that claims for pure economic loss can succeed. The requirements for such a cause of action, which is typically brought against professional advisers for negligent advice, are

- a close and direct relationship between the parties
- reasonable foreseeability of damage, and
- that it is fair, just and reasonable to impose liability.

(See further *Hedley Byrne and Co. v. Heller and Partners Ltd* which concerned a duty in relation to the provision of information upon which the provider knew, or ought to have known, that the recipient would rely.)

Trespass to land

An action for trespass to land can be brought by a person entitled to possession of the land against a person whose unlawful act causes direct physical interference with the land. Thus, where polluting matter is released into a river so that it passes downstream and settles on land, the person in possession of that land may bring an action in trespass against the polluter. However, the threshhold for such claims is very high. First, the act which results in the trespass must be deliberate or intentional – even though the trespass itself may be unintentional – and secondly the interference must be direct. It is rather unclear what 'direct' means in this context but it appears to require a causal link between the deliberate act and the inevitability of its consequences. This means that to succeed in a trespass action for water pollution, for example, it would be necessary to demonstrate that polluting matter poured into a stormwater drain would inevitably flow directly into a nearby stream causing pollution. Despite a few cases in which trespass has been used as a successful remedy to pollution incidents (see *McDonald v. Associated Fuels* and *Jones v. Llanrwst UDC*) it is not a frequently used cause of action.

If it were not for the strict interpretation of 'direct interference', trespass might prove a very useful form of action in relation to pollution cases, because it is only necessary to show that there has been direct interference with a person's common-law rights, not that actual damage has occurred. In this respect, trespass has the potential to play a more active role in pollution prevention than the other common-law rights of action, as it creates the possibility of getting an injunction before *actual* environmental damage occurs.

1.4. WHO'S WHO IN ENVIRONMENTAL LAW?

This Section aims to provide a brief summary of the key players in the field of environmental law in the UK. This task has been greatly simplified following the enactment of the Environment Act 1995, which established the Environment Agency and transferred to it the powers, duties and assets of the National Rivers Authority, Her Majesty's Inspectorate of Pollution and the local Waste Regulation Authorities.

1.4.1. The Environment Agency

The Environment Agency came into being on 1 April 1996 and is one of the largest organisations in the world charged with environmental regulation, with some 9500 staff and an annual budget of nearly £600m. Its 'one-stop shop' approach was intended to make environmental regulation in the UK more integrated, for the benefit of the individuals and businesses whose activities are regulated, and the environment.

The Agency has taken on the responsibilities formerly associated with its constituent parts, namely

- management of water resources (NRA)
- pollution control in respect of water resources (NRA)
- flood defence (NRA)
- regulation of waste management (WRAs)
- regulation of the most polluting industrial processes (HMIP).

Essentially the Agency determines applications for most types of environmental consent, e.g. Waste Management Licences. It has powers to require remediation of pollution and, in default, to carry out the work itself and recoup the cost of doing so from the polluter or land owner. It also has the power to prosecute offenders.

The Agency has published an *Enforcement and Prosecution Policy* which sets out the general principles which the Agency intends to follow in relation to enforcement and prosecution (consistency, transparency etc.), and this is used in conjunction with more detailed specific guidance relating to particular offences and breaches, the 'Functional Guidelines'. These guidelines set out a national system for recording and categorising pollution incidents and assessing the appropriate level of enforcement response. The 'Common Incident Classification Scheme' (CICS) classifies incidents in four categories

- Category 1 – a major actual or potential environmental impact

- Category 2 – a significant actual or potential impact
- Category 3 – a minor actual or potential impact, and
- Category 4 – no actual or potential environmental impact.

The CICS is then supplemented by different methods of enforcement applicable to each of the Agency's functions, i.e. environmental protection, fisheries, water resources, flood defence and navigation. There is an individual section for each, which sets out

- the purpose of enforcement for that function
- the enforcement powers available
- the factors determining enforcement action
- enforcement for non-criminal non-compliance, and
- the various criminal offences and enforcement options.

If an incident is of significant actual or potential impact (Category 1) then a prosecution will usually result. If it is Category 2, then prosecution or Formal Caution will be the usual course of action, the choice being determined by other factors set out in the Guidelines. If it is Category 3, then a warning will usually be sufficient unless other factors determine a more severe course of action, e.g. repeat offence. From a contractor's point of view, the Functional Guidelines are a useful indicator of the Agency's likely response in the event of a pollution incident, but as with most guidelines, there will always be scope for exceptions and deviations.

The Environment Agency, however, does not have total control of all environmental regulation; the Drinking Water Inspectorate still remains a separate body, and the Agency does not have any direct functions relating to nature conservation, although it has a number of general duties relating to sites of nature conservation interest. In addition, certain regulatory powers remain with local authorities, such as administration of the new statutory clean-up regime for contaminated land (see Chapter 4) and regulation of those industries deemed to be less polluting under the system of Integrated Pollution Prevention and Control (IPPC) – for further details about this system see Section 1.4.2 below and Chapter 2 (Section 2.2.3).

In addition the Agency acquired new responsibilities under the Environment Act 1995, including

- administration and regulation of the producer responsibility initiative in respect of packaging waste
- being statutory consultee in respect of the National Waste Strategy and the National Air Quality Strategy
- carrying out research and providing information on the environment
- issuing guidance in respect of matters such as IPC processes and contaminated land, and perhaps most importantly
- a special advisory role in respect of contaminated land remediation, which falls largely within the remit of local authorities, and is discussed in more detail in Chapter 4.

1.4.2. Local authorities

On a day-to-day level practical decision-making and enforcement in relation to environmental legislation often falls to local government officers. In particular, the following issues are dealt with by local authorities

- control of noise from premises including control of noise from construction sites pursuant to ss.60 and 61 of the Control of Pollution Act 1974
- town and country planning (see Section 1.4.3 below)
- land-use history (based on planning registers)
- public health matters
- statutory nuisance (the law in this area is set out in Part III of the EPA 1990, and described in more detail in Chapter 7)
- waste collection and disposal
- regulatory responsibility for the control of smoke, dust, grit and fumes under the Clean Air Acts and related legislation
- regulation of the less polluting industrial processes which are covered by Part I of the EPA 1990, under the regime known as Air Pollution Control. In this context local authorities liaise with the Environment Agency in relation to the more polluting industrial processes, regulated under the EPA 1990 Integrated Pollution Control regime, and are responsible for maintaining the public registers for IPC and APC for all those businesses which are authorised under Part I of the

EPA 1990 within their area. This dual system of control is in the process of being replaced by a single system of control under the Integrated Pollution Prevention and Control (IPPC) Act 1999 (see further Chapter 2, Section 2.2.3). Local authorities also control the less polluting installations under IPPC (for either all environmental impacts, known as Part A(2) installations, or just atmospheric emissions, known as Part B installations)

- under the statutory clean-up regime for contaminated land, local authorities are responsible for inspecting for the existence of and identifying contaminated land within their area, and then for taking action against the person responsible for the contamination or the owner/occupier of the land. They are assisted in part by the Environment Agency. This regime is described in some detail in Chapter 4.

1.4.3. Local planning authorities

The other important 'environmental' function performed at local government level is that of the local planning authority. Planning authorities have a number of roles in relation to planning policy and development control, namely

- determining applications for development consent, e.g. planning permission and listed building consent, at first instance
- responsibility for related matters such as tree preservation orders, listed building protection, conservation areas, hazardous substances consents, the control of derelict land, and the protection of the countryside, including wildlife and habitats
- the preparation of development plans, containing strategic policies relating to such matters as transport, housing, employment and other land uses. This is a particularly important function, because s.70(2) Town and Country Planning Act 1990 states that in dealing with an application for planning permission the planning authority shall have regard to the provisions of the development plan, so far as it is material to the application, and to any other material considerations, and s.54A TCPA 1990 provides that

where in making any determination under planning legislation regard is to be had to the development plan, and the determination shall be made in accordance with the plan unless material considerations indicate otherwise. This creates a plan-led development regime and it is therefore important that planning authorities ensure their plans are accurate and up to date

- determining whether a proposed development should be subject to an Environmental Impact Assessment
- keeping a register, available for inspection by the public, showing details of all current applications, and past decisions including planning permissions
- taking enforcement action in respect of breaches of planning control.

The local planning authorities are primarily the District Councils. The County Councils also have planning functions, being responsible for

- the preparation of structure plans, strategic development plans for the wider area
- preparation of waste and minerals plans, and
- determining applications in respect of minerals extraction and waste disposal or treatment.

However, the London Boroughs, the Metropolitan Authorities and in some cases now the Unitary Authorities (in many cases created by the devolution of a District Council from a County Council area), carry out both sets of planning functions described above.

1.4.4. Water and sewerage undertakers

The privatised water and sewerage companies have three key functions

- maintenance of sewerage systems and sewage treatment works
- provision of drinking water for public consumption, and
- regulation of trade effluent discharges to sewer.

Section 118 of the Water Industry Act 1991 requires that any discharge of trade effluent into an undertaker's sewer must be made in accordance with a formal consent from that sewerage undertaker, who can specify conditions to which that consent will be subject, such as the nature and composition of the discharge, and its temperature and pH.

Most sewage treatment works discharge to controlled waters. Where this is the case the sewerage undertaker will require a discharge consent from the Environment Agency. The sewerage undertaker therefore requires to ensure that the consents that it grants to industrial customers will not cause it to breach its own discharge consent.

1.4.5. The Secretary of State for the Environment, Food and Rural Affairs

The Secretary of State for the Environment, Food and Rural Affairs has three main functions in relation to environmental law

- promoting legislation for the regulation of environmental issues
- issuing policy guidance to assist regulators, the regulated and interested third parties in understanding legislation and government policy, for example through Circulars, Guidance Notes and Codes of Practice
- determining appeals against the decisions of regulatory bodies such as the Environment Agency.

2

The planning process

2.1. INTRODUCTION

The extent to which the planning process will be relevant to the construction industry will vary enormously from project to project. Traditionally contractors have tended to become involved in a development project once any environmental impact studies have been carried out and the relevant planning permissions are in place. However, with the growth in number of Private Finance Initiative (PFI) schemes, and other forms of contract which involve a greater transfer of risk and responsibility to the contractor in the early stages of the project, the role of the contractor is changing. Increasingly, contracts are structured so that the contractor will have responsibility for making the planning application and acquiring the necessary licences for the development. Even where contractors are not directly responsible for obtaining planning consent for a development, all building works must be carried out in accordance with the relevant permissions, and so an understanding of the process is, at the very least, desirable.

Where the proposed development has the potential to have an adverse effect on the environment either during the construction phase, or once it is an operating facility, it will probably be subject to one or more of the pollution control regimes which function separately from planning control. For this reason this Chapter contains a brief section at the end on the interaction between planning and pollution control. However, in practice the two systems tend to run in parallel, and the pollution control regimes, such as those governing contaminated land (Chapter 4), waste (Chapter 5) and water (Chapter 6) are intended to complement the planning process in that they are all effectively designed to protect the environment from the potential risk posed by development.

2.2. PLANNING APPLICATIONS, PERMISSIONS AND OTHER CONSENTS

When planning permission is required
Section 1.4.3 gives a brief introduction to local planning authorities, and this Section will focus on which developments will require planning permission, how to go about making an application and what to expect in terms of costs, delays and negotiations.

Whether the involvement is with a development for a potentially hazardous operation such as a waste incinerator, or a small housing development, planning permission will be required before work can commence. In broad terms, planning permission is required for any development of land. The Town and Country Planning Act 1990 (s.55(1)) provides the following definitions.

- 'Development' is 'the carrying out of building, engineering, mining or other operations in, on, over or under land, or the making of any material change in the use of any buildings or other land'.
- 'Building operations' will include demolition of buildings (subject to the paragraph below on demolition); erection of new buildings; structural alterations of, or additions to, buildings; and other operations normally undertaken by a person carrying on business as a builder.

Demolition of buildings does not require planning permission in every case, although it is included within the definition of 'building operations'. The Town and Country Planning (Demolition – Description of Buildings) Direction 1995 (Appendix A to DoE Circular 10/95 Planning Controls over Demolition) states that only the demolition of dwelling houses, buildings adjoining dwelling houses and buildings whose cubic content exceeds 50 cubic metres, is to be taken to involve development requiring planning permission. Listed buildings, buildings in conservation areas and scheduled ancient monuments cannot, however, be demolished without consent under the statutes which regulate them. Demolition of any other type of building is permitted under the Town and Country Planning (General Permitted Development) Order 1995. Notwithstanding that demolition does not require planning permission there is a requirement that prior notification of demolition should be given to the local planning authority which has the power to decide on the method of demolition and proposals for site restoration. The only exceptions to this requirement for referral to the local planning authority are in emergency cases (where written justification must be provided to the local planning authority as soon as reasonably practicable) and where a planning permission or planning order includes demolition.

Planning permission must generally be obtained by means of an application by the developer to the local planning authority with responsibility for the area within which the development site lies. Certain types of small-scale or non-controversial development – such as the creation of hardstanding within the boundary of industrial premises – may not require express permission or, therefore, an application to be made, as they may be covered by a 'blanket' deemed consent under the Town and Country Planning (General Permitted Development) Order 1995 (which is amended from time to time). However, express planning permission will generally be required for the majority of development work.

If a building is of special architectural or historic interest it may be 'listed' by the Secretary of State. Local planning authorities designate areas of special architectural or historic interest as conservation areas. Both listed buildings and buildings in conservation areas are given special protection in law and listed building consent and/or conservation area consent under the Planning (Listed Buildings and Conservation Areas) Act 1990 will be required in addition to planning permission if such buildings are to be the subject of building works.

Who may make an application?

Anyone may submit an application for planning permission regardless of any ownership rights, but where the applicant is not the sole owner of the site in question, notice must be served on the owner and any tenants of the land with more than a seven-year leasehold interest, in order to ensure that they are aware of the application and enable them to make representations to be taken into account by the local planning authority, if they wish. Having given notice, the applicant must complete a certificate stating what notices, if any, have been served, and this certificate must then be submitted to the authority with the application.

2.2.1. How to make an application

Under the Town and Country Planning (Applications) Regulations 1988, an application for planning permission must be made on a form provided by the local authority. It must include a plan showing the site to be developed edged in red, together with details of the proposed development. This information is then submitted to the planning authority, who may ask the applicant for further information or verification of certain aspects of the application. However, it is advisable to have pre-submission discussions/negotiations with the local planning authority regarding any significant development proposal.

Fees are payable for all applications for planning permission, and there are fixed charges for different types of application which are set out in the Town and Country Planning (Fees for Applications and Deemed Applications) Regulations 1989 and their subsequent amendments. A telephone call to the local planning authority is usually the easiest way to discover the current rates for different types of development. No fee is payable in relation to applications for listed building or conservation area consent.

In some cases, it is possible to get outline planning permission for a site, which means that the local authority approves the development in principle, but reserves judgement in respect of one or more of the following matters

- siting
- design
- external appearance
- means of access
- landscaping of the site.

Outline permission still necessitates an application to the local planning authority, and payment of a fee, as for full planning permission. Furthermore, it is necessary to apply for subsequent approval of 'reserved matters' within three years – or any other period stipulated by the local authority – of the grant of outline permission, or it will lapse. Having granted outline planning permission, the local authority may not subsequently refuse to approve any of the reserved matters because of objections to the development itself. In other words, in granting outline planning permission, the authority has accepted the concept of the development, albeit not the details. For this reason, local authorities may be reluctant to grant outline permissions without full details of certain key factors, such as the external appearance and means of access to the development.

Outline permission is only available for building operations – as opposed to engineering or mining operations or a material change in the use of land – but it can be helpful to establish the principle of consent for the proposed development. This in turn can prove a useful carrot to attract finance for the development, particularly in cases where the site itself is of little value, being derelict or contaminated, for instance.

Planning Policy Guidance Note 23, which deals with the interaction between the planning and pollution control regimes, makes it clear that an outline permission will not usually be appropriate where the development is likely to entail the risk of significant pollution. This means that where an Integrated Pollution Control (IPC)/Integrated Pollution Prevention and Control (IPPC) authorisation (see Section 2.2.3) or a Waste Management Licence (see Section 5.2.3) is required for operation of the development, an application for a full planning permission will usually have to be made. Similarly an outline planning application may not be appropriate where an Environmental Impact Assessment (see Chapter 3) is required to ascertain the likely significant environmental effects of the proposed development. Such effects cannot be assessed if there is only limited information contained within the planning application and there is insufficient certainty about what is to be developed in due course.

2.2.2. How the decision is made

In determining an application for planning permission the local planning authority (or the Secretary of State on appeal) is required to have regard to central government planning policy which is issued in the form of Circulars and Planning Policy Guidance Notes (PPGs), and the provisions of the local development plan and any regional plans such as waste or mineral plans. While the local authority has a wide discretion whether or not to grant planning permission, that discretion must be exercised on grounds of planning policy.

PPGs

PPGs set out central government policy on planning and so are a material consideration in the local authority's decision-making process, and should therefore be considered where relevant. The list of currently available PPGs is available in the form of The Consolidated List of National Planning Policy, which can be found on the DTLR website (www.databases.dtlr.gov.uk/planning/npp/ListCategories.asp). Whatever the nature of a development, there will be a number of PPGs whose guidance is likely to be relevant; an understanding of central government policy combined with an appreciation of the local development plan increase a planning application's chances of success.

In the context of contaminated land, for example, PPG 14 is likely to be one of the most relevant sources of guidance. PPG 14 is concerned with developing land which is unstable or potentially unstable, and is intended to ensure that any development on such land is suitable and that physical constraints on the land are taken into account at all stages of planning. This means that any scope for remedial, preventive or precautionary measures should be fully explored. PPG 23 is also helpful in this context in that it offers guidance on determination of planning applications for land which might be contaminated. For more information about the development of contaminated land, see Chapter 4.

Development plans

Local planning authorities are required to prepare development plans in respect of their areas, and anyone wishing to submit a planning application should first study the relevant plan for the area in which the proposed development is to be located. The local authority has a duty to determine the application in accordance with the provisions of the development plan, to the extent that it is relevant, unless material considerations dictate otherwise (s.70(2) TCPA 1990).

The purpose of a development plan is to set out the strategy for development in the area concerned. Development plans are not prescriptive, rather they lay down policies, aims, objectives and goals. Plans should be reviewed at least every 10 years, through a system of public participation and consultation. Although plans have no immediate effect other than as a statement of what the local authority considers desirable, where a developer or would-be developer owns or has an option on land within an area in which the development plan is in the process of being reviewed, the developer would be well advised to make representations in respect of his preferred end-use for the site. If he succeeds in getting his site zoned appropriately for his intended development, a subsequent application for planning permission stands a greater chance of success. Section 54A of the TCPA 1990 and PPG 1 introduce a presumption in favour of development which is in accordance with the development plan. A developer who proposes a development which clearly conflicts with the development plan would need to demonstrate why the plan should not prevail. It is therefore important to have an understanding of the plan when preparing the application either to demonstrate that the development is in accordance with the plan or that there are good reasons why it is not.

For most areas the development plan consists of two tiers, the structure plan and the local plan, but in areas served by a unitary authority, unitary development plans combine the functions of both structure plan and local plan. However, the planning authority will give guidance as to the documents which make up the development plan for the particular area concerned. These will be in written and drawn plan form.

In addition to structure and local plans, some areas may also be subject to minerals local plans and waste local plans. The minerals local plan will contain the mineral planning authority's detailed policy for winning and working minerals within its area or the deposit of mineral waste. The relevant authority will normally be the county council, although in metropolitan areas it will be the unitary authorities.

In areas with a two-tier local government system the waste local plan also comes within the county council's remit and simply sets out the planning authority's policies on waste. Such policies should be consistent with the Environment Agency's waste disposal plans, which set out the arrangements which are in place for treating and disposing of controlled waste so as to prevent or minimise pollution of the environment or harm to human health. Waste disposal plans do not address land use issues as a development plan does, but they may provide useful information about the Environment Agency's local policies in respect of waste regulation and availability of disposal facilities. An amended version of PPG 10 on Planning and Waste Management now contains up-to-date Government policy on the relationship between planning and waste management, an earlier version of which was contained within PPG 23. PPG 23 has been significantly depleted by this removal of sections relating solely to waste management, but as it was issued in 1994 and a full review has been repeatedly delayed, it is now quite out-of-date in any event. PPG 10 should be read in conjunction with the newly-issued PPG 11 on regional planning. Waste regulation is discussed in more detail in Chapter 5.

2.2.3. Conditions and planning obligations

When a local planning authority grants planning permission for development it has the power to impose conditions on that permission. There will almost always be a condition requiring that the development begins within a specified period, usually five years (in the case of full consent) or requiring the submission of details for approval of 'reserved matters' within three years (in the case of outline consent), failing which, permission lapses. In fact, if there is no express condition to this effect, the five- and three-year time limits are implied by statute, pursuant to ss. 91 and 92 of the TCPA 1990.

Almost invariably the local planning authority will impose other conditions to ensure that the development is carried out in an acceptable manner. Conditions may, for example, regulate the materials to be used in the development, methods or hours of working, detailed layouts, the phasing of works and many other matters. Planning conditions or 'section 106 agreements', outlined below, can also provide legally-binding mechanisms to ensure that risks from contaminated land, for example, are expressly dealt with at the expense of the landowner or developer applicant. Conditions should only be imposed if they are necessary, relevant, enforceable, precise and reasonable in all other respects. Failure to observe or comply with a condition is a breach of planning control and the local authority has a range of enforcement measures which it can take.

As well as imposing conditions it is open to the local planning authority to require an applicant for planning permission to enter into a planning obligation. These obligations, which can be entered into as agreements or unilaterally by the developer, are commonly known as 'section 106 agreements'. They allow the local planning authority to secure from developers binding contractual obligations that run with the land, where they consider it necessary to do so to overcome some harm which would otherwise arise from a proposed development, or to provide some benefit to the locality, effectively as the 'price' for planning permission. So, for example, if the approach roads to a site are considered to be inadequate the local planning authority can require an obligation on the part of the developer to contribute to road improvements.

The power to require such obligations is quite wide. An obligation may

- restrict the development or use of the land in any specified way
- require specified operations or activities to be carried out in, under or over the land
- require the land to be used in any specified way, or
- require a sum or sums of money to be paid to the local planning authority.

Where the applicant for planning permission is not the owner of the land, but planning permission will only be granted subject to entering into a planning obligation, it will be necessary to persuade the landowner to enter into the obligation to bind the land. Planning obligations are registered as local land charges.

Where the local planning authority considers that a planning obligation is required, it will not generally issue a planning consent until the agreement has been agreed and executed.

2.2.4. Highways and other agreements

In addition to the s.106 agreements to which Section 2.2.3 refers, there are other situations which can involve developers entering into agreements with the local authority or the local water company to enable a development to proceed. The three most common types of agreement are as follows:

- In the case of a new housing estate, for example, a developer may enter into an agreement pursuant to the Highways Act 1980 in order that the new estate roads are maintained by the local highway authority. This is known as a 'section 38 agreement'.
- Where a development entails the alteration of road junctions or roundabouts on existing highways, for example, and the alterations are being carried out for public benefit, the developer may be required to contribute all or part of the construction costs, by way of a section 278 agreement with the highway authority.
- A developer who is to provide a development with sewers which are to form part of the public sewer network will enter into an agreement with the local water company under s.104 of the Water Industry Act 1991.

2.2.5. Appeals

The local planning authority is obliged to determine an application for planning permission within eight weeks of receipt (or within 16 weeks where the application is accompanied by an Environmental Impact Assessment) unless a longer period has been agreed with the applicant in writing. If the application is not determined within this period, the applicant may treat the failure to determine as a deemed refusal and has the right to appeal to the Secretary of State. In practice, it is not unusual for determinations to take longer than eight weeks.

An applicant can also appeal to the Secretary of State where the local planning authority has refused planning permission or has granted it subject to conditions which the applicant considers unacceptable or onerous or when an enforcement notice has been served on him.

An appeal to the Secretary of State amounts to a total reconsideration of the application and may take the form of a public inquiry, written representations, or an informal hearing. Most appeals are dealt with by way of written representations, but large-scale or complex appeals are more likely to be dealt with at public inquiry, and any party to an appeal can insist that a public inquiry be held.

The decision on such an appeal to allow or refuse the planning permission, or attach conditions, is generally delegated by the Secretary of State to an inspector, but in certain circumstances the inspector's report can go to the Secretary of State in order that the latter can make a final decision in light of the former's recommendations. Unlike most civil litigation, parties to a planning appeal are expected to pay their own costs unless there has been 'unreasonable behaviour' by one of the parties which justifies an award of costs against them. For guidance on what constitutes 'unreasonable behaviour', see DoE Circular 8/93.

2.2.6. Enforcement of development controls

If development is carried out without planning permission or in contravention of any conditions imposed on a planning permission there is a breach of planning control. Where it appears to a local planning authority that there has been a breach of planning control, it may take enforcement action provided that it does so within the time limits set out in s.171B TCPA 1990. It has four years to enforce breaches involving operational development (from the date of their substantial completion) or changes of use to a single dwellinghouse, and ten years from the time of the breach in all other cases. It is possible to apply to vary a condition on a planning permission if the circumstances of a development change, but once the four-year or ten-year enforcement period has expired there would be little point as the local planning authority could no longer take enforcement action so the development would effectively have permission in any event.

The local planning authority will generally serve an enforcement notice under s.172 TCPA 1990, specifying the alleged breach, the steps required to remedy it or the problems it has caused, and the time within which those steps must be carried out. Non-compliance with an enforcement notice in the absence of an appeal to the Secretary of State (see Section 2.2.5) is a criminal offence.

If the person on whom an enforcement notice is served appeals to the Secretary of State, he may continue to operate notwithstanding the alleged breach of planning control, until that appeal is determined. If the local planning authority wishes to prevent this from happening it may serve a stop notice under s.183 TCPA 1990, although if this turns out to be unjustified, compensation may be payable. It is a criminal offence not to comply with a stop notice.

If there is a breach of a condition attached to a planning permission the local planning authority may serve a breach of condition notice on the person carrying out the development or the person who has control of the land. There must be compliance within 28 days, failing which a criminal offence will be committed. There is no appeal to the Secretary of State from a breach of condition notice. Not complying with such a notice leads to a maximum fine of £1000.

Local planning authorities can also apply to the courts for an injunction to restrain actual or potential breaches of planning control.

2.3. PLANNING AND POLLUTION CONTROL

The Department of the Environment published PPG 23: *Planning and Pollution Control* (referred to above), in an attempt to clarify the boundaries between the regimes and to prevent duplication of statutory controls. Planning controls are not intended as a means of regulating polluting activities, except where they are applied in the context of storage of hazardous substances, which is covered by the Planning (Hazardous Substances) Act 1990 and the Planning (Hazardous Substances) Regulations 1992. However, this legislation is unlikely to be relevant unless what is involved is the storage of large quantities of hazardous substances, far in excess of the typical quantities of substances which are traditionally found on a construction site. The safe storage and handling of toxic and corrosive substances of the type usually found on a construction site are discussed in Chapter 7, but for more detailed information on this subject, see *Masons' Guide: Health and Safety Law for the Construction Industry.*

In order to prevent duplication of controls, or inadequacy of controls, consultation between planning authorities and pollution control authorities is very important. PPG 23 suggests that such consultation should take place as early as possible on receipt of an application, in order that each body has a full appreciation of factors which might influence the decision-making process one way or another. For this reason, those responsible for obtaining planning permission for a development as well as any environmental consents are generally advised to submit applications for everything at the same time, in order to facilitate liaison between the relevant authorities and, hopefully, speed up the granting of the necessary consents.

However, it is recognised that an applicant will not always have sufficient information to make an application for an IPC/IPPC authorisation, for example, at the same time as his planning permission, and in such cases, a staged application for the IPC/IPPC authorisation is an option which allows an element of prior discussion with all the relevant authorities, and should enable matters to progress more effectively than if various applications are made over a period of time.

It should be noted though, that while IPC authorisations and

WMLs cannot be granted in the absence of a valid planning permission, an IPPC authorisation is an exception to this rule. There is no requirement to obtain planning permission for any development associated with an application for an IPPC permit, prior to obtaining that permit, or vice versa. However, in practice there will generally be close links between the assessment of environmental impacts under the planning regime and under IPPC.

Typical construction activities – such as demolition, excavation, piling and cladding – are not designated as prescribed processes and it is therefore unlikely that those undertaking traditional construction projects will ever have any involvement with the IPC/IPPC regime. However, as construction companies become more involved in schemes which consist of both building and operating, the relevance for them of the IPC/IPPC regime may grow. The licensing regimes which operate in respect of water and waste, and which are likely to be much more familiar to the construction industry, are dealt with in detail in Chapters 5 and 6.

Part I of the Environmental Protection Act 1990 introduced the IPC system which was aimed at improving the regulation of industrial processes. Part I in fact consisted of two separate systems

- IPC covering the more polluting processes, regulated by the Environment Agency and intended to prevent or minimise pollution of any environmental medium, and
- Air Pollution Control (APC) controlling solely atmospheric emissions from the less polluting processes, and regulated by the local authority's environmental health department.

A fundamental change to this legislation has now been brought into force so as to implement the EU Directive (96/61/EC) on integrated pollution prevention and control (IPPC). In order to superimpose the IPPC system onto an already established and complex regime, Part I of the EPA 1990 is being repealed. It is being replaced with a new system, chiefly contained within the Pollution Prevention and Control Regulations 2000 (PPC Regulations), which came into force on 1 August 2000.

Although largely inspired by the UK's IPC system, IPPC will involve some changes:

- The range of environmental impacts covered by IPPC is wider than for IPC, which was essentially focussed on emissions. For example, IPPC requires that measures be taken on closure of a site to avoid any pollution risk and to restore the site to a satisfactory state. IPPC also regulates noise and vibration, and requires that energy be used efficiently.
- IPPC applies to many more installations than IPC. The Government has estimated that in addition to the 2000 processes currently regulated under IPC and the 2500 processes covered by APC, some 1000 landfill sites, 1000 intensive pig and poultry farms and about 500 food and drink factories will be brought within the IPPC regime.
- IPC regulates about 400 processes which are not caught by the IPPC Directive, but they will continue to be regulated under the UK's implementation of IPPC.

The PPC Regulations, like Part I of the EPA 1990, make it a criminal offence for any person to operate a prescribed activity except in accordance with an authorisation granted by the regulator. Although Part I will eventually be replaced entirely by the new regime, until all the processes have been phased into IPPC (2007), Part I will continue to be relevant.

Schedule 1 of the PPC Regulations contains the list of controlled activities, divided into six categories

- the energy industry (fuel production processes, combustion processes (including power generation))
- metal production and processing
- minerals industries
- the chemicals industry
- waste management, and
- other industries.

Those involved in making an application for IPPC authorisation should be aware that it is a demanding regime which generally requires significant resources and should not be undertaken without the necessary technical expertise.

3

Environmental impact assessment

3.1. INTRODUCTION

For certain types of development, a detailed assessment of the likely environmental impact will be required, and this will be a material consideration for the planning authority determining the inevitable application for planning consent. The Town and Country Planning (Environmental Impact Assessment)(England and Wales) Regulations 1999 (the EIA Regulations) came into effect on 14 March 1999 and replace the Assessment of Environmental Effects (England and Wales) Regulations 1988. The revised EIA Regulations reflect the requirements of Directive 97/11/EC and introduce a number of procedures designed to make the EIA decision-making process more transparent for all those involved.

The EIA Regulations stipulate for which types of project an environmental impact assessment should be a component of the decision-making process. Projects are categorised into Schedule 1 – projects for which environmental assessment is compulsory – and Schedule 2 – projects for which environmental assessment is at the discretion of the local planning authority or, in certain circumstances, of the Secretary of State. In addition to projects listed in the EIA Regulations, there is a growing incidence of developers volunteering some kind of 'environmental statement' even where it is not specifically required by the local authority, because it is felt that such information will assist their planning application, by possibly heading off certain areas of potential difficulty or sensitivity.

3.2. ENVIRONMENTAL IMPACT ASSESSMENT IN PRACTICE

3.2.1. Whether an assessment is required

Determining whether a project will require an Environmental Impact Assessment (EIA) is generally straightforward. Schedule 1 projects include significant infrastructure developments such as motorways and major roads, thermal power stations, chemical installations and special waste disposal installations; in other words, the kinds of project which one would expect to be scrutinised thoroughly and to be the subject of a major planning inquiry. Where there is any doubt about whether or not a project falls within Schedule 1, a ruling on the point can be obtained from the Secretary of State or the local planning authority.

Schedule 2 projects tend to be less sensitive in nature than those in Schedule 1, and include mineral extraction, food manufacture, holiday villages, wastewater treatment plants and rendering plants. Such projects will not automatically require an EIA; the local planning authority has the discretion to require one only where developments 'are likely to have significant effects on the environment by virtue of factors such as their nature, size or location'. The significance of the environmental effects is decided by the local planning authority on a case-by-case basis, according to government guidelines. Understandably there is no statutory definition of 'significant effects on the environment', although DETR Circular 2/99 provides general guidance on how to assess 'significance' and sets out three general criteria by way of guidance

- where the project is of more than local significance in terms of its size and physical scale
- where the development is to be sited in an environmentally-

sensitive or vulnerable location, such as a national park or site of special scientific interest

- where the project is likely to give rise to unusually complex and potentially hazardous environmental effects.

In addition to these three general criteria, the Circular sets out specific thresholds and criteria for each category of Schedule 2 project, which essentially relate to the size and scale of the project, or the area of land that will be utilised. However, such thresholds and criteria are only intended to be used as a guideline, and in practice each project will be looked at individually.

Where a proposed development may require an EIA, developers are advised to consult the relevant planning authority well in advance of a planning application. A 'screening opinion' on whether an EIA is needed in a particular case can be requested from the planning authority as soon as certain basic information can be provided about the proposal. Such information must include

- a plan identifying the proposed development site
- a brief description of its nature and purpose, and
- its possible effects on the environment.

The planning authority must give its opinion within three weeks, unless the developer agrees to a longer period. A developer who is dissatisfied with the planning authority's opinion may refer the matter to the Secretary of State, who will then normally give a direction within three weeks of the developer's application.

Where a project does require an EIA, the local planning authority or the Secretary of State must provide a written statement giving clear and precise reasons for its opinion. Both this statement and the developer's application will be made available for public inspection.

Earlier criticisms relating to inconsistency between local authorities in determining when an EIA is required have been addressed in part by the introduction of the formal screening process for Schedule 2 projects. Government guidance available in the form of Circular No. 2/99 is also intended to improve consistency in this context, as well as to assist in the preparation of an Environmental Statement.

3.2.2. The Environmental Statement

EIA is a process which involves an assessment undertaken by the local planning authority on the basis of environmental information supplied to it. This information consists in part of an Environmental Statement prepared by the developer (or more usually, by hired consultants), and other information supplied by various statutory consultees (for examples of these see Section 3.2.3 below), independent third parties (such as local conservation and amenity groups), members of the public and even the local planning authority itself.

Where a project requires an EIA it is the developer's responsibility to prepare the Environmental Statement which is then submitted with the planning application. Its preparation should be a collaborative exercise involving discussions with the planning authority, statutory consultees and possibly other bodies as well.

Consideration should be given individually to both the construction and operational phases of the development, as the environmental impacts arising from these two distinct stages are likely to be different. An Environmental Statement should deal primarily with the significant effects to which the project might give rise; it is not intended to cover every conceivable environmental impact of the project. However, it is important that agreement is reached with the local planning authority as to the pertinent issues before beginning work on the Environmental Statement. Environmental Statements will need to be scoped according to the type of project in question; a proposal for a nuclear power station would obviously require a much more detailed review of alternative sites than a proposal for a poultry farm, for example.

The EIA Regulations enable a developer – before making a planning application – to ask the planning authority for a formal 'scoping opinion' on the information to be included in an Environmental Statement. A scoping opinion is effectively the local planning authority's interpretation of the information required by the EIA Regulations (see below) in the context of the proposed development. A scoping opinion is not a mandatory requirement. The developer may also wish to submit a draft outline of the Environmental Statement, both to indicate what the developer considers the main issues to be and to provide a focus for the authority's consideration. The authority must consult certain bodies and the developer before issuing a scoping opinion, and must issue the opinion within five weeks of receiving the request. If the authority fails to issue a scoping opinion within five weeks, or any extension agreed with the developer, the developer may apply to the Secretary of State for a scoping direction. However, there is no appeal provision where the authority and developer disagree about the content of the Environmental Statement.

The Environmental Statement will comprise a document, or series of documents containing certain specified information enabling an assessment of the likely impact on the environment of the proposed development. Schedule 4 to the EIA Regulations lists the information which an Environmental Statement should contain, which can be summarised as follows

- a description of the proposed development and site, and details of its design, size and scale
- a description of measures intended to avoid, minimise or remedy any such significant adverse effects which are identified
- the data required to identify and assess the main effects which the development is likely to have on the environment
- an outline of the main alternatives considered by the applicant, and the reasons for which the proposed development is preferable
- a summary of the information specified above, in non-technical language.

Schedule 4 goes on to state that the Environmental Statement may also include further information by way of explanation or amplification, such as

- the physical characteristics and land-use requirements of the proposed development, both during its construction and operational phases
- details of the production processes to be operated and the nature and quantity of materials to be used, where appropriate
- details of the emissions and waste products which will result from the development when operational, and their likely direct and indirect effects on the environment

- a description of the development's likely significant effects on the environment, both direct and indirect, with reference to humans, flora, fauna, soil, water, air, climate, landscape, material assets and cultural heritage
- any difficulties encountered with providing the specified information, such as lack of relevant scientific data or technical knowledge.

A summary of any such additional information should also be provided using non-technical language.

3.2.3. Preparing statements

In practical terms, preparation of an Environmental Statement tends to be a significant undertaking:

- A project manager will be required to co-ordinate input to the Environmental Statement, as it is likely to involve contributions from more than one consultant or specialist, and in some cases projects will involve a whole team of experts to address a variety of impacts, from the project's effect on the local natterjack toad population to the question of skyline changes.
- Careful drafting and presentation of the Environmental Statement will be very important to the success of the planning application.
- The involvement of a lawyer at an early stage in the production of the Environmental Statement is recommended, both to assist with interpretation of the statutory guidance — application of the threshold criteria, for example — and to perform an editorial role, pulling together the various inputs, in order to ensure that the Environmental Statement is a balanced and coherent document, so as to minimise the risk of challenge. Even if a challenge is unsuccessful it is likely to delay the project, which may result in additional expense.

The consultation exercise, which is often extensive, is fundamental to the whole EIA process. In gathering information for the Environmental Statement, one is expected to consult not only the local planning authority, but also statutory, and possibly non-statutory, consultees. The requirement for the developer/applicant to consult relevant statutory bodies is found in Regulation 12 of the EIA Regulations. The local planning authorities have similar obligations once they are in receipt of the Environmental Statement (Regulation 13).

Regulation 13 of the EIA Regulations provides that the statutory consultees include, where appropriate

- the Health and Safety Executive
- the Environment Agency
- the Highway Authority
- English Heritage
- English Nature
- the Department for the Environment, Food and Rural Affairs, and
- the relevant Nature Conservancy Council.

Examples of non-statutory consultees would include the RSPB, CPRE, local conservation groups and members of the general public. If the project is likely to be subject to local opposition, wide-ranging consultation at an early stage of the development can be a useful indicator of sensitive issues, and may help to minimise conflicts later. Local planning authority decisions should take account of public consultations and the principal reasons behind decisions should be made public.

3.2.4. Submitting the statement

Once the Environmental Statement is complete, it is submitted with the planning application and the authority then has an extended period of 16 weeks (as opposed to an eight-week period for non-EIA applications) in which to determine the application. However, in practice, the average determination period tends to be about 36 weeks, with some applications taking over a year to be determined. Compared with a standard planning application, there are greater requirements for publicity; the developer must ensure that the planning application, and the Environmental Statement are advertised in full in the local newspaper, and in a site notice.

Where the planning authority feels that the Environmental Statement is inadequate it has powers to request further information. Clearly in producing the Environmental Statement every effort should be made to minimise the risk of such requests, in order to avoid further delay and expense. If a developer fails to produce further information and the local authority decides to refuse planning permission, or fails to determine the application within the 16-week period, the developer has the usual right of appeal to the Secretary of State.

As there are currently no agreed standards or methodology for assessing environmental impacts, the quality of Environmental Statements produced varies widely. However, this is an area of practice which is slowly 'maturing' and the 1999 Regulations provide a means of achieving a greater level of certainty through the introduction of scoping opinions. Government guidance available in the form of Circular No. 2/99 is also intended to improve consistency in this context, as well as assist in the preparation of an Environmental Statement by setting out certain general requirements and the procedures to be followed. Nonetheless, there is no substitute for good professional advice.

In this context there are a growing number of centres of excellence for EIA both in the UK and internationally. The Institute of Environmental Management and Assessment has published a number of documents which provide practical guidance including 'Guidelines for Baseline Ecological Assessment' and 'Guidelines for Environmental Assessment of Road Traffic', both of which can be ordered from www.iema.net. A number of academic institutions also have a wealth of research material available. Oxford Brookes University Impact Assessment Unit produces regular Practice Updates, and Working Papers, one of which Screening, Scoping and ES Review under the 1999 Environmental Impact Assessment Regulations [2000] is helpful in that it covers the amended regime, whereas much of the available guidance material pre-dates the 1999 Regulations. Aberystwyth University also has a specialist EIA Unit (see www.aber.ac.uk).

4

Contaminated land

4.1. INTRODUCTION

Concern over the risks associated with contaminated land has been growing steadily over the past 20 years, and for the construction industry it is becoming an increasingly important issue as planning authorities seek to encourage developers to utilise brownfield sites in preference to greenfield. The risk of unforeseen ground conditions, the question of whether some form of clean-up is required, and issues of liability arising from ownership or occupation of a contaminated site, as well as from activities to be carried out on site, are all important considerations for those involved in construction and development projects. Contaminated sites have the potential to require consideration of almost all of the issues raised in this book.

- In certain circumstances contaminated land has the potential to give rise to tortious liability in respect of nuisance, negligence, trespass and the rule in *Rylands v. Fletcher* (Chapter 1).
- The planning authority will be concerned to ensure that any proposed use or development of a contaminated site will not give rise to unacceptable risks to health or the environment. Planning powers are intended to complement, not substitute, pollution control legislation (Chapter 2).

- When working on a contaminated site, waste materials may require handling and disposing of with particular care, and certain remediation operations will require a Waste Management Licence (Chapter 5).
- Contaminated sites may pose a threat to nearby ground and surface waters, and this threat may be exacerbated by construction practices which do not take account of the risks involved (Chapter 6).
- Protection of employees and others on site may be relevant where soil or building structures contain substances hazardous to health (Chapter 7).
- Special insurance arrangements may be needed in respect of works taking place on a contaminated site, and lending institutions may require additional assurances by way of detailed site surveys and soil testing before being prepared to commit to a project on a contaminated site (Chapter 8).

It will often become known during the planning stage of a development that a site contains polluting material. In that case a developer should warn the contractor at the tender or pre-qualification stage, in order that the contractor has adequate time to consider how he will handle, store and dispose of contaminated soil, water or gaseous emissions, how he will protect his workforce, what his on-going liabilities in respect of the site may be — if any — and how these additional risks will be reflected in the contract price.

Where the nature of the site is unknown, contractors should be aware of the significant costs which could be incurred if unforeseen contaminants are encountered on site, not least because civil engineering contracts in particular tend to be based on the assumption that the contractor will have inspected the site and be aware of the ground and subsoil conditions. For example, Clause 11(2) of the *ICE Conditions of Contract* (7th Edition) states that the contractor shall be deemed to have examined the site, its surroundings and all relevant available information, and that he is reasonably satisfied that he has obtained the necessary information as to the risks which may influence or affect his tender.

Having determined that a site may present increased levels of risk as a result of contamination, careful thought should be given to apportionment of that risk between the parties involved. In practice, a contractor may have little choice about the way in which related risks are apportioned, but where liability for contamination is a realistic possibility, insurance to cover unforeseen ground conditions or environmental impairment should be considered. Insurance for pollution risks is discussed further in Chapter 8.

In addition to consideration of the contractual framework for the project, the statutory regime in this context is potentially very significant, even though a formalised legal framework to deal with the remediation of contaminated sites has only recently come into effect. The Environment Act 1995 contains a series of amendments to the EPA 1990 which should assist local authorities — who have been given the primary responsibility for cleaning up contaminated land in the UK — and the Environment Agency — which operates in an overseeing capacity — in determining which sites are candidates for immediate attention and from whom the costs of clean-up might be recovered.

Although before the introduction of this new regime a range of statutory and common law remedies was potentially available to tackle contaminated land in certain circumstances — and indeed, has been utilised in this context — Part IIA of the EPA 1990 has attracted considerable media attention because it is the first piece of legislation which is specifically aimed at remediation of contaminated land. The relationship between the new regime and alternative statutory and non-statutory remedies is discussed further at Section 4.3 below.

Part IIA of the EPA 1990 came into force on 1 April 2000. Local authorities are required to take a strategic approach to inspection of land within their area (see Section 4.2 below) with a written strategy being produced within 15 months of the issue of the guidance, ie. by the end of June 2001. This approach was to enable local authorities to identify land meriting detailed inspection, ascertain which sites required most urgent attention and where resources should be prioritised. However, this 15-month 'planning' period means that it is still too early to assess the practical application of the new regime.

4.2. THE NEW STATUTORY FRAMEWORK

The statutory basis of the new regime
The statutory basis of the regime, as already mentioned, is Part IIA of
the EPA 1990. This is supplemented by statutory guidance which is to
be found in Annex 3 of the extensive DETR Circular 02/2000
entitled 'Contaminated Land' which consists of six Annexes which set
out Government policy, an outline of the regime, a guide to the
Regulations and the Commencement Order, and a glossary of
relevant terminology. Though long, the Circular is essential reading
for an understanding of the practical application of the regime, with
the statutory guidance in Annex 3 being the most important element
because of its statutory status.

The local authority's duty to identify contaminated land
The new regime creates a duty on every local authority to inspect land
within its area 'from time to time' with a view to identifying
contaminated land. This will be land which appears to the local
authority to be in such a condition by reason of substances in, on or
under it, that

- significant harm is being caused or there is a significant possibility
  of such harm being caused, or
- pollution of controlled waters is being, or is likely to be, caused.

The definition of 'significant harm' is provided in Annex 3 of the
accompanying statutory guidance. It suggests that only the most
severely contaminated sites are likely to fall within the first and more
vague of these two limbs of the definition of contaminated land.
The second limb, being more specific, is less open to interpretation
but it has in turn, caused concern on account of the fact that the
risk-based approach which is adopted in respect of pollution of soil,
is not utilised in relation to actual or potential pollution of
controlled waters. Whereas the impact on people, property, plants
and wildlife must be 'significant' to fall within the definition of
'contaminated land' and trigger the clean-up regime, *any* pollution

of controlled waters would be sufficient, as there is no qualifying threshold relating to the significance of the pollution. Indeed, amendment of the primary legislation would be required to establish a threshold for 'significant' water pollution, and this would then be inconsistent with the 'anti-pollution works' provision which exists under s.161A of the Water Resources Act 1991 (see Section 6.3). However, the water pollution in question does have to be a present phenomenon, not a past event, for the land to be classed as 'contaminated land'.

The remediation notice
When the local authority identifies such a site, it must notify certain interested parties, namely the Environment Agency and what is known as the 'appropriate person(s)'. When a site is identified as being contaminated, the local authority must decide what steps need to be undertaken to improve the condition of the site, and the appropriate person will then be notified by means of a remediation notice as to the required remediation and the time limits within which the work must be carried out.

In the first instance, the appropriate person will be the person who *caused or knowingly permitted* the contamination (such people are known as Class A persons), but if, and only if, the whereabouts of this person are unknown, the appropriate person is the current owner or occupier of the land (known as Class B persons). It follows from this definition of 'appropriate person' that

- there may well be situations where there are two or more people who might be considered 'appropriate' for the purposes of this legislation; in such cases, the authority has a discretion to apportion liability. Where there are two or more appropriate persons in relation to the same remediation action, s.78F(6) (EPA 1990) requires the enforcing authority to determine, in accordance with the statutory guidance, whether any of them might be excluded from the liability group. However, the complexity of the exclusion procedure, coupled with the fact that it is as yet untested in practice, takes it outside the scope of this Guide. Those interested to know more should look at s.78F and the related ss.78J and 78K, and then DETR Circular 2/2000, Annex 3, Chapter D which specifically deals with the exclusion from and apportionment of liability;

- it is not inconceivable that a contractor occupying the site for the term of his contract could be deemed an appropriate person either as an occupier (Class B) or as a Class A person if, for example, he either introduces hazardous substances to a site which subsequently lead to contamination of soil or controlled waters, or he mobilises existing contaminants to exacerbate pollution on site, or on adjoining land.

In fact, the procedure is neither as automatic nor as harsh as this summary may make it seem to be. The reasons for this are as follows:

- A period of at least three months' advance warning of the intention to serve a remediation notice must be given – this is intended to allow for a period of consultation. It would be wise to use this period to seek to avoid the notice being served either by drawing relevant circumstances to the attention of the enforcing authority, or by putting forward a voluntary scheme for remediation.
- Where the authority is satisfied that things are being or will be done by way of remediation, the notice will not be served.
- Similarly, if the cost of the clean-up is too high relative to the seriousness of the contamination, the notice should not be served.
- The guidance suggests that only the most severely contaminated sites are likely to fall within the first limb of the definition of 'contaminated land', although the second limb relating to the potential of land to pollute controlled waters may be more easily triggered, as discussed above.
- Risk assessment is an essential ingredient when determining whether land is 'contaminated' and the guidance establishes the concept of 'pollutant linkages'. A pollutant linkage consists of a contaminant (the source), a relevant receptor (the target) and a possible pathway between the two. The pathway represents the

route through which the contaminant is, or could be, exposed to the receptor. Unless all three elements of a pollutant linkage can be identified, land should not be classed as 'contaminated land'. In other words, an almost legal approach to proof of a causal link and some potential damage is required – speculation is not a sufficient basis for imposing this kind of liability.

- In determining what harm is 'significant', the condition of the land in question is to be assessed in relation to the current use of the land, or of any land which might be affected, and should be consistent with the 'suitable for use' approach set out in the DoE *Framework for Contaminated Land: 'Paying for Our Past'*. This document essentially advocates a risk-based approach; for example, a high level of clean-up will be required where a site is to be developed for residential use – where there could be a risk to children playing in gardens – but where the site is to remain in industrial use, or is to be concreted and used for car parking, the level of clean-up required will be considerably lower.

Costs of compliance or non-compliance with remediation notice
Where a remediation notice is served and the required remediation will necessitate landfill disposal of contaminated material from the site, the recipient will not be able to apply for a remediation exemption from the Landfill Tax. (See further Appendix A of Information Note 1/97 on Reclamation of Contaminated Land, published by HM Customs and Excise.) The cost implications of this obviously provide another reason to engage with the relevant authority prior to service of a notice.

Failure to comply with a notice is an offence. Where the notice relates to industrial, trade or business premises the appropriate person shall be liable on summary conviction to a fine of up to £20 000, and a further fine of up to £2000 per day for each day that the offence continues after conviction. Failure to comply with a notice in respect of other premises is an offence punishable by a fine of up to £5000 and a daily fine of up to £500 for each day that the offence continues after conviction. Where the recipient of a notice fails to comply with its terms, the relevant authority has the power to carry out remediation works, and recover its reasonable costs from that person.

One of the most significant issues which arises out of the new contaminated land framework is the fact that the potential liability, in terms of remediation costs, is unlimited.

Furthermore, there is no specified point in time in the new legislation beyond which a potential 'appropriate person' might be free to consider himself beyond the reach of the regulator in respect of a contaminated site. Responsibility as an *occupier* is relevant, of course, only during the period of occupation; but responsibility as a polluter — i.e. as a Class A appropriate person — can continue indefinitely.

Clearly the extent to which the regime is utilised will vary from one local authority to another and will depend on the nature of the area over which each authority presides. Nonetheless it seems likely that unless the contamination poses a threat to a watercourse, the regime is only likely to apply to the more seriously contaminated sites.

4.3. FURTHER STATUTORY AND NON-STATUTORY LIABILITIES

While contractors occupying a contaminated site may be considered 'appropriate persons' in certain circumstances and possibly even find themselves subject to a remediation notice which can entail substantial liabilities, this is not their only point of exposure in respect of contaminated land.

- The Environment Agency has widely-drafted powers to prevent, remedy or mitigate pollution of controlled waters under the Water Resources Act 1991, and could require the owner or occupier of contaminated land, or the person who caused or knowingly permitted the water pollution, to remediate such land where it represents a source of water pollution, or alternatively the Agency can seek to recover its costs from such persons where it has carried out anti-pollution works to prevent or remediate water pollution (see Section 6.3).

- Although the Environment Act 1995 amends s.79 of the EPA 1990 to preclude any land in a 'contaminated state' from being a statutory nuisance — in order to ensure consistency with the new regime — matters such as stenches caused by deposits of substances on the land, can still constitute a statutory nuisance. The statutory nuisance provisions are intended to provide local authorities and individuals with a quick and easy remedy to abate nuisances (see Section 7.3).

- Although probably of less direct relevance to the construction industry, another source of potential contaminated land liability is the new IPPC regime, discussed at Section 2.2.3 above. In theory there should be no overlap between IPPC and the new contaminated land regime because they are separately regulated with different objectives and approaches, but in practice comparisons are likely to be made. Basically, if the site report submitted with an IPPC application does not include details of historic pollution or other non-IPPC pollution, any contamination present when the IPPC authorisation is later surrendered, will be deemed to be IPPC pollution and subject to the post-closure IPPC clean-up provisions. However, IPPC imposes a much higher clean-up standard than the contaminated land regime, as the former requires the site to be returned to its condition prior to the issue of the IPPC permit, as opposed to the new regime which imposes a clean-up standard of 'suitable for use'.

Potential non-statutory liabilities for contaminated land include those under contract. Contractors, engineers and other professionals familiar with the development or remediation of contaminated sites will be aware of the pressure from clients to take on significant levels of risk in respect of contamination. In addition to clean-up costs under a remediation notice, other liabilities which can result from contractual risk allocation of this kind — whether through indemnities to the client in respect of his liability or warranties to third parties — include

- liabilities to persons taking an interest in the property in the future, such as tenants and funders as well, of course, as future purchasers, and
- in effect, liabilities to third parties in tort.

Furthermore, the potential liabilities which clients are seeking to transfer in this way are not always limited to liability for pollution specifically caused by the works being undertaken on site. Some clients may seek to offset liability for historic pollution which manifests itself at some time in the future.

Clearly the level of risk that a contractor is prepared to accept – and at what cost – is a commercial decision for the individual or company concerned. The short point is that risks arising from the state of the land require careful and specific consideration. In additional to the risks faced by contractors in their traditional role, the Private Finance Initiative approach to contracting is blurring the distinction between landowners, contractors and professional advisers, because it involves various combinations of professionals as members of consortia bidding for projects and therefore performing much more the role of developers. In general terms, the closer one comes to having an interest in or control over the occupation of land, the greater the exposure to front-line risks in respect of pollution.

In the context of long term contracts such as those which underpin PFI projects, the approach of government departments and other bodies such as healthcare trusts varies as to their chosen method of apportioning the risk of environmental liabilities. Some seek to provide the bidding consortia with a certain amount of environmental information for the purposes of tendering procedures (although in practice the information that is available may be far from adequate). The successful or preferred bidder will also have the opportunity to raise enquiries and carry out such investigations in relation to the site as are necessary. This is particularly important where the development or project is to be constructed on land in the vicinity of abandoned or disused mines or on other types of environmentally-polluted sites.

The contractor will then be expected to accept the risk of managing any potential liabilities which he may face, and the costs inherent in eradicating them as part of the carrying out of the works, on the basis that he has been made aware of them and has been given the opportunity to price them. In general, it is accepted that the risk of environmental compliance rests exclusively with the contractor under most PFI projects, unless he is able to negotiate something to the contrary.

In addition to contractual liabilities, it is important to be aware of the risk of common-law tort actions in the context of contaminated land. For example, it may be possible to bring an action in private nuisance on grounds that contamination has caused a substantial and unreasonable interference with the use of adjoining property. As in the case of the new statutory regime outlined above, the person liable would be the person actually responsible for causing the nuisance, or if that person could not be found, the liability could fall on the owner or occupier of the site causing the nuisance though only if he has a degree of knowledge of or involvement in the pollution. Similarly other liabilities might arise in negligence or for breach of statutory duty, although the likelihood of success of each of these causes of action would depend on the specific circumstances of the contamination. For further information about the possible impact of the common law as a means of environmental control, see Chapter 1.

5

Waste management and the landfill tax

5.1. INTRODUCTION

In addition to being a generator of large quantities of waste, the construction industry is also responsible for a high level of innovation in the area of reuse and recycling of by-products and secondary materials. While materials which are to be reused may not be regarded as 'waste' by a contractor who can put them to good purpose, it is always necessary to consider such materials in the context of the statutory framework for waste management. This Chapter will look at circumstances in which it may be necessary for a contractor to obtain a Waste Management Licence (WML) for a site, how to apply for one, and the legal issues associated with the day-to-day management of waste on site during the period of a contract.

Another issue which should be considered by the contractor before commencing work on site is the landfill tax and its financial implications for a project. A development scheme or engineering project which involves significant quantities of waste material being taken off-site for disposal — albeit inert substances such as soil or rock — will incur substantial costs for transportation and disposal of the waste, which will be increased further by the impact of the landfill tax. This Chapter will look at the operation of the landfill tax, and the extent to which its impact might be minimised in certain

59

circumstances through the judicious reuse and recycling of waste materials as part of the development project.

5.2. SUMMARY OF THE WASTE MANAGEMENT REGIME

Section 5.2.1 deals with the definition of 'waste'. In circumstances where the material in question is particularly hazardous, it may also be classed as 'special waste' and be subject to more stringent regulation. The definition of special waste and an outline of its regulation – which is essentially the same as for less hazardous waste, with additional obligations in respect of its transportation and labelling – are included at Section 5.2.2. If the material in question is waste, and it is not exempt, a contractor who is involved in disposing of it or recovering it will usually be required to apply for a WML – see Section 5.2.3. The relevant exemptions are set out in Section 5.2.4, and special considerations relating to the surrender of WMLs are discussed in Section 5.2.5.

Where a project simply involves the generation of waste materials which are passed to a registered carrier for disposal, a contractor will not require a WML, although he will still need to comply with the Duty of Care which applies to all those who import, produce, carry, treat, keep or dispose of waste or, as brokers, have control of such waste. The Duty of Care is an 'umbrella' obligation which overarches all those dealing with waste in any capacity, regardless of whether they are subject to a WML, within one of the exemptions, transporting waste on- or off-site, or handling special waste. Its implications are discussed in Section 5.2.6.

Particular requirements apply in respect of the transportation of waste which, together with details about relevant documentation, are set out in Section 5.2.7. The requirements covering movement of special waste are included in Section 5.2.2.

For information on the disposal of liquid waste to sewers, see Section 6.4.

5.2.1. The definition of 'waste'

Waste in the UK is defined in the Waste Management Licensing Regulations 1994, by reference to the European definition which is established by Council Directive 75/442/EEC as amended by 91/156/EEC. This defines waste as 'any substance or object ... which the holder discards or intends or is required to discard'. As a consequence, waste in the UK is now referred to in the context of 'Directive waste' and this terminology replaces all references to 'controlled waste', which pre-dates the introduction of the concept of 'Directive waste'.

The definition of Directive waste should be considered in conjunction with the European Waste Catalogue which lists various types of waste, and includes, for example, 'construction and demolition waste' (referenced in the Catalogue as 17 00 00) and 'soil and dredging spoil' (referenced as 17 05 00). In seeking to determine whether or not something falls within the definition of Directive waste, therefore, a reasonable approach would be to consider

- first, the perspective of the holder — does he intend to discard the material in question?
- second, the material in question — is it included in the European Waste Catalogue?

There will be materials that are to be discarded or given away by their present holder, which are not specifically covered in the European Waste Catalogue (e.g. milk bottles put out for doorstep collection would not fall within the definition of Directive waste). Similarly, inclusion of a particular substance or object in the European Waste Catalogue does not mean that it will be waste in all circumstances — where the producer or person in possession of the material does not intend, or is not required, to discard it, it will not normally be waste.

This concept of 'discarding' and the wider definition of waste constitute an extremely complex area of law which is continually being refined by the UK courts and the European Court of Justice. As a starting point it is worth referring to the extensive guidance provided by DoE Circular 11/94 which suggests that to determine whether a substance or object has been discarded, the following question may be asked;

> '*Has the substance or object been discarded so that it is no longer part of the normal commercial cycle or chain of utility?*'

The guidance suggests that if the answer to this question is 'no', this should be a reasonable indication that the substance or object concerned is not waste. The Circular provides the example of glass bottles which are subject to a refundable deposit on safe return. The DoE contends that the bottles are not waste in the hands of the buyer, the shop to which they are returned or the supplier who collects them from the shop. In these circumstances the bottles never leave the 'chain of utility'. On the other hand, bottles which are placed in a 'bottle bank' for recycling are discarded and should be treated as waste.

The Circular goes on to provide further clarification of the concept in four broad categories of potential waste

- worn but functioning substances or objects which are still usable (albeit after repair) for the purpose for which they were made — generally not waste
- substances or objects which can be put to immediate use without requiring a specialised waste recovery establishment or undertaking — generally not waste
- degenerated substances or objects which can be put to use only by establishments or undertakings specialising in waste recovery — generally waste even if transferred for value
- substances or objects which the holder does not want and which he has to pay to have taken away - depends on the facts of the particular disposal. Where there is an intention that the subject or object will be used by the recipient and no special recovery process is required — generally not waste, notwithstanding that a price is paid.

While the detailed guidance set out in the Circular must be regarded as persuasive in that it represents the considered view of the executive of one of the Member States, an authoritative interpretation of 'Directive waste' is ultimately a matter for the courts. Recent case-law has clarified certain points, and confused issues such as the status of recovered material, so some analysis of relevant case-law is necessary.

English case-law based on the definition of waste under the Control of Pollution Act 1974 (COPA 1974) held that, in broad terms, waste is defined from the perspective of the person in possession of the material in question. To this extent it was consistent with the European definition, although lacking the additional dimension of the European Waste Catalogue which, since its introduction in 1994, extends the definition of waste to include a consideration of the material in question. The cases discussed below were based on s.3 of COPA 1974 which defined 'waste' from the perspective of the person discarding the material, so they are still helpful in establishing key principles useful in interpreting 'Directive waste'. In the following cases, the defendant companies were prosecuted for breach of COPA 1974 and sought to demonstrate that the material in question was not waste.

- In *Kent CC v. Queenborough Rolling Mill Co. Ltd* the defendant company filled an area subject to subsidence with a mixture of ballast, china, china clay and broken pottery from a disused site which was being cleared by a demolition company. On appeal, the Divisional Court held that although the material was put to a useful purpose, that was not relevant in deciding that the material was waste. The important issue was the nature of material when it was discarded; if it was waste at that point, it would remain so until it was adequately reconstituted or recycled. The secondary point – the fact that waste can cease to be waste when it is recovered – was recently reaffirmed by the High Court in *Mayer Parry Recycling Limited v. Environment Agency* (see below).
- The Court formed a similar view in *Meston Technical Services Ltd and Wright v. Warwickshire County Council* where the defendants operated a waste recycling business and traded in liquid controlled waste which they reprocessed into substances to be sold for commercial use or disposed of by way of landfill or incineration. On appeal the defendants argued that the material was not waste because they could recycle or reuse it and it was therefore valuable to them. Secondly, if they did not regard it as waste and intended to sell it on if they could, they could not be guilty of an offence. The Divisional Court held that the value of the material and the views of the defendant were irrelevant when considering the definition of waste, and it was not appropriate

to examine the aims and purposes of the holder when considering what was waste under the Environmental Protection Act 1990 (EPA 1990). The new, wider definition of 'Directive waste' would support this interpretation of 'waste'.

- In *Cheshire CC v. Armstrong's Transport (Wigan) Ltd* the defendant company processed building site rubble and then returned the crushed material to its original site to assist in rebuilding works. The Court held that the material was a product and not therefore waste. The defendant was able to demonstrate that there was no intention to discard on the part of the previous holder of the material as the defendant company was under a contractual obligation to return the material to site once it had been processed. On appeal, this decision was upheld and the Divisional Court held that the contractual obligation meant that the rubble was not waste as the original holder had not wished to dispose of it. In essence it is necessary to show that the material has not left the 'chain of utility'.

Certain broad principles can therefore be drawn as to what constitutes 'waste' in the context of the construction industry.

- Waste is defined from the perspective of the person in possession of the material in question. If that person discards, or intends to discard, the material, then it will qualify as waste.
- If material is waste in one person's hands and discarded, it will be treated as waste by the regulators even if it is subsequently used as raw material and is of value to a third party.
- Where a party has material from its site processed elsewhere and returned to the site for use for a new purpose it will not have discarded the material which will therefore not be waste.
- Where material is required by contract to be utilised for some new purpose on a site from which it originates it will not be waste.

More recent case-law has focussed on whether material which has been 'discarded' has been consigned to a waste recovery or a waste disposal operation. In *Mayer Parry Recycling Limited v. Environment Agency* Mr Justice Carnwath relied on two high profile opinions of Advocate-General Jacobs (*Euro Tombesi* and *Inter-Environnement*

Wallonie v. Regione Wallonie) when he stated:

> '*Materials which are to be re-used (rather than finally disposed of), but which do not require any recovery operation before being put to their new use, are not treated as waste.*'

However, as the Advocate-General's opinion was not endorsed by the European Court of Justice's judgments in these two cases, and the later decision of *Arco-Chemie Nederland* was similarly inconsistent, it has now been held that Mr Justice Carnwath's decision in *Mayer Parry* should not be followed. In *Attorney-General's Reference 5/2000* the Court of Appeal held that condensate produced by an animal rendering plant and spread on land as a fertiliser remained waste even though it had not been subject to any recovery operation. It would now seem that unless the framework Directive is amended, recovery or disposal operations as listed in the Directive are not required before a substance can be controlled waste. Similarly, waste which is intended for some form of recovery operation only loses its status as 'waste' once it has finished going through one of the recovery operations listed in the framework Directive, and not before (*Castle Cement v. Environment Agency* [2001]).

The one thing that is clear from the case-law is that there is a very fine divide between material which is classed as waste and that which is not, and the definition tends to be applied on a case-by-case basis. For this reason it would be unwise for a contractor to assume that he is *not* dealing with 'waste' without first seeking legal advice. Even then, he may not get a very clear answer.

5.2.2. Special waste

'Special waste' can be loosely defined as those substances which are particularly hazardous to the environment or public health, and disposal of which is dangerous or difficult. The relevant provisions governing these types of waste are contained within the Special Waste Regulations 1996 which came into force on 1 September 1996, and their subsequent amendments. These Regulations replaced the Control of Pollution (Special Waste) Regulations 1980, and transpose into UK legislation the Hazardous Waste Directive. In practice special waste is defined as any waste which is listed in Part I of Schedule 2 of the Special Waste Regulations (e.g. construction and demolition waste; paints; varnishes; adhesives and sealants etc.) and which displays any of the properties specified in Part II of that Schedule. Such properties include

- explosive
- oxidising
- flammable
- irritant

- harmful
- toxic
- carcinogenic
- corrosive

- infectious, and
- eco-toxic.

The types of wastes covered by the Regulations therefore include acids, alkaline solutions, asbestos, pharmaceutical compounds, industrial solvents, fly ash, pesticides, batteries, waste oils and photographic chemicals.

While contractors and other construction professionals may come into contact with special waste in the context of site debris or material to be incorporated into the works, excavation or remediation works on a contaminated site are much more likely to involve handling special waste. Many contractors will be used to dealing with asbestos, and will be familiar with the Control of Asbestos at Work Regulations 1987 and their amendments, but should be aware that there is also specific legislation governing other types of special waste. The procedure for dealing with special waste parallels that for dealing with all forms of Directive waste under the EPA 1990 – discussed in Sections 5.2.3–5.2.7 below – although the system of coded consignment notes which governs the movement of special waste is more complex than that for ordinary wastes.

The Special Waste Regulations 1996 are intended to bring about greater accountability of those responsible for special waste, and will apply to anyone who produces, handles, treats or disposes of special waste. Pursuant to the Regulations, the Environment Agency must be notified at least three working days in advance of any consignment of special waste being moved for disposal. This includes movements of waste to and from sites such as storage and treatment facilities, in addition to movements to final disposal sites. Particular care should obviously be taken by contractors who are responsible for storing special waste on site, both to protect employees and to prevent harm to the environment.

The Regulations introduce a system of coded consignment notes intended to provide better descriptions of wastes and to create an 'audit trail' that will enable the Environment Agency to monitor the movement of special waste from the point where it is produced to its point of final disposal. A charge — £15 (November 2001) — is made for each consignment which is intended to offset some of the Agency's costs. Failure to comply with the Regulations could result in an unlimited fine and/or up to two years in prison if convicted in the Crown Court. In the event that there is a breach of the requirement to obtain a WML in respect of special waste, the penalties on conviction are more severe, and can be punished by fines and/or imprisonment for up to five years.

5.2.3. Waste Management Licences

The WML is the central pillar of the provisions contained within Part II of the EPA 1990, the Act which underpins the legal framework surrounding the control of waste in the UK. Before the waste management licensing regime came into force from 1 May 1994, licences were granted under COPA 1974 and were known as Waste Disposal Licences.

Section 33 of the EPA 1990 states that a person shall not:

(a) deposit controlled waste, or knowingly cause or knowingly permit controlled waste to be deposited in or on any land unless a Waste Management Licence authorising the deposit is in force and the deposit is in accordance with the licence;
(b) treat, keep or dispose of controlled waste, or knowingly cause or knowingly permit controlled waste to be treated, kept or disposed of:
(i) in or on any land, or (ii) by means of any mobile plant, except under and in accordance with a Waste Management Licence;
(c) treat, keep or dispose of controlled waste in a manner likely to cause pollution of the environment or harm to human health.

Most of the provisions of the EPA 1990 refer to 'controlled waste' which is defined as meaning household, commercial or industrial waste. However, the term 'controlled waste' and its definition have been amended, as mentioned above, by the Waste Management Licensing Regulations 1994, and replaced by the single category of 'Directive waste'.

An application for a licence for the treatment, keeping or disposal of waste in or on land should be made in writing to the Environment Agency office in whose area the site is situated. An application for mobile plant should be made to the Environment Agency office in whose area the operator has his principal place of business; in this way a number of pieces of plant can be covered by one licence. Only the occupier of the land, or the mobile plant operator may apply for a WML, and although there is no definition of 'occupier' in the EPA 1990, it is presumably linked to the ability to control the waste operation and the use of the land.

If the Environment Agency considers the applicant to be a 'fit and proper person' it cannot reject the application, unless granting it would cause pollution to the environment, harm to human health or serious detriment to the amenities of the locality. The only exception to this rule is where planning permission is required for the use of the land, and such permission has not been granted. The definition of a 'fit and proper person' is defined at s.74 of the EPA 1990 in the negative; an applicant shall be treated as *unfit* to hold a WML where

- the applicant or another relevant person has been convicted of a relevant offence, or
- the management of the site will not be in the hands of a technically competent person, or
- the applicant cannot make adequate financial provision to discharge the obligations arising from the licence.

A list of 'relevant offences' is contained within the Waste Management Licensing Regulations 1994. However, under the EPA 1990, s.74(4), the Environment Agency has the discretion to ignore a conviction if it chooses to do so. This means that a person may have committed a relevant offence and still be treated as a fit and proper person if the Agency chooses to overlook the offence. Guidance on these provisions is contained within Chapter 3 of Waste Management Paper No. 4: Licensing of Waste Management Facilities. It is possible to be deemed a 'fit and proper person' in respect of one type of facility — such as a small mobile plant — but not another, such as a major landfill site. The requirement to be technically competent refers to the person responsible for the day-to-day management of the waste facility, and for the vast majority of sites, a person is only 'technically competent' if he holds the relevant certificate of technical competence awarded by the Waste Management Industry Training and Advisory Board (WAMITAB).

The Environment Agency has a wide discretion to attach 'appropriate' conditions to the licence although, unlike many pieces of environmental legislation, the EPA 1990 does not provide a list of the types of conditions which are appropriate. Guidance is given, however, in Waste Management Paper No. 4, which stresses that conditions should relate to the operation and management of the site, so as not to duplicate conditions attached to the planning consent. The Paper also states that conditions should be enforceable, unambiguous, necessary and comprehensive, and that operators should know exactly what they need to do to comply with them.

Section 43 of the EPA 1990 contains wide-ranging rights of appeal to the Secretary of State. An applicant may appeal where

- an application for a licence is rejected, or not determined within four months
- the licence is subject to onerous conditions
- the conditions are modified by the Environment Agency
- an application to modify the conditions is rejected, or not determined within two months
- the licence is suspended or revoked
- an application to surrender the licence is rejected, or not determined within three months, or
- an application to transfer the licence is rejected, or not determined within two months.

In accordance with the 'polluter pays' principle, a system of fees and charges exists in respect of WMLs intended to recover the Environment Agency's costs associated with processing an application and supervising a licence. In order to ensure that different operations pay a fair charge relative to one another, a fairly complex scheme has been implemented. Activities which are subject to a WML are divided into four main categories

- treatment of waste
- keeping of waste
- disposal of waste, and
- situations where a site has closed and a certificate of completion is sought (see Section 5.2.5 below).

These categories are then sub-divided to take account of whether waste is to be reused or recycled, and then the various charges are worked out with reference to factors such as the type of waste involved, e.g. household waste, special waste etc., and (where the licence is for the operation of a waste receiving site) the amount of waste a site is licensed to take annually. There are separate fees for initial licence applications, and for applications to transfer, modify or surrender respectively. There is also an annual subsistence charge to be paid, and so fees and charges will usually be in the order of several thousand pounds, depending on the nature of the facility.

5.2.4. Exemptions

Even though material may be classified as 'waste', there are certain circumstances in which such material may be kept, treated or disposed of without the need for a WML. The Waste Management Licensing Regulations 1994 contain a long list of exemptions to the requirement to obtain a WML, and these can be summarised into seven broad categories as follows

(a) activities which are already regulated in accordance with consents or licences granted under other legislation; for example, an Integrated Pollution Prevention and Control authorisation (see Section 2.2.3)

(b) storage of waste at its place of production pending its removal for treatment or disposal elsewhere, provided that the producer can demonstrate that it will be collected

(c)   storage of 'special waste' at its place of production pending its removal for treatment or disposal elsewhere, provided that certain conditions are met relating to quantity and security

(d)   certain activities relating to the recovery or reuse of waste, such as sorting, baling, shredding or compacting it at its place of production

(e)   various activities intended to encourage recycling of waste, such as the collection of paper and cardboard, aluminium and steel cans, plastics, glass and textiles for recycling, and the cleaning of packaging for its reuse, subject to detailed restrictions on quantities

(f)   deposit of certain organic matter for the purposes of fertilising or conditioning land, and

(g)   storage or disposal of construction or demolition waste for the purposes of construction work being undertaken on the land.

Exemptions to the waste management licensing regime are all subject to detailed conditions, and do not usually apply where the waste is 'special waste'. These seven categories are a broad summary of Schedule 3 of the Waste Management Licensing Regulations 1994 which consists of 45 paragraphs, each of which describes specific circumstances in which waste may be managed in such a way so as to be exempt from the requirement to hold a WML. Those paragraphs which are thought to be most likely to be of relevance to the construction industry, in that they fall broadly within category (g) above, are described below.

Paragraph 7 of Schedule 3 creates an exemption where waste soil, compost, wood, bark and other plant matter is spread on land which is used for agriculture, in quantities up to 250 tonnes per hectare in any twelve-month period, provided that it results in benefit to agriculture or ecological improvement.

Paragraph 9 exempts the spreading on land of 'waste consisting of soil, rock, ash or sludge, or of waste from dredging any inland waters or arising from construction or demolition' where it is to be used for the reclamation or improvement of that land. This exemption is likely to be relevant to contractors in certain circumstances, but there are certain limitations to its application

- for reasons of industrial or other development, the land must be incapable of beneficial use without treatment
- planning permission is required for the reclamation or improvement of the land
- the spreading of waste must result in benefit to agriculture or ecological improvement, and
- spreading is limited to a maximum of 20 000 cubic metres per hectare.

Paragraph 13 exempts the manufacture of timber products, straw boards, plaster boards, bricks, blocks, roadstone or aggregate where they are made from

- demolition or construction waste, or
- waste which consists of ash, slag, clinker, rock, wood, bark, paper, straw or gypsum.

The manufacture of soil or soil substitutes from any of these materials is also exempt, provided that the manufacture takes place either at the point of production of the waste, or where the material is to be applied to land, and the total amount manufactured does not exceed 500 tonnes in any one day.

Paragraph 13 also exempts the treatment of waste soil or rock which is to be spread on land, provided that the treatment takes place either at the point of production of the waste, or where the material is to be applied to land, and the total amount treated does not exceed 100 tonnes in any one day.

Waste which is stored for the purpose of any of the activities listed in Paragraph 13 is also exempt, assuming that it is stored at the place where the activity is carried out, and does not exceed 20 000 tonnes, or 50 000 tonnes in the case of road planings to be used to make roadstone.

Paragraph 19 permits ash, slag, clinker, rock, wood or gypsum arising from construction or demolition work, tunnelling or other excavations, to be stored on site where it is suitable for 'relevant work' on that site, or it may be stored for up to three months before work commences where it is not produced on site. Up to 50 000 tonnes of road planings may be stored for up to three months if it is to be used elsewhere. 'Relevant work' means construction work and includes the deposit of waste on land in connection with the provision of recreation facilities, or the construction, maintenance, or improvement of a building, highway, railway, airport, dock or other transport facility on that land, but excludes other forms of waste disposal and land reclamation work.

Paragraph 24 exempts 'the crushing, grinding or other size reduction of waste bricks, tiles or concrete' where these activities are subject to an authorisation granted under Part I of the EPA 1990, or an IPPC permit granted under the Pollution Prevention and Control Regulations 2000, dealing with mineral processing.

Paragraph 27 exempts the bailing, compacting, crushing, shredding or pulverising of waste at the place where it is produced, as well as its storage at the site prior to one of these operations.

Paragraph 35 exempts waste consisting of mineral material excavated from a borehole or other excavation, provided that the purpose is mineral excavation and the material is deposited on site, not exceeding 45 000 cubic metres per hectare in any two-year period.

All these exemptions are subject, in addition, to the following conditions

- the activity must be carried on with the consent of the landowner where it takes place
- the person carrying on the activity must otherwise be entitled to do so on that land
- the waste must be recovered or disposed of without harm to human health or the environment
- specifically there must be no risk to water, air, soil, plants or animals
- the activity must not cause a nuisance through odours or noise, and
- the activity must not adversely affect the countryside or places of special interest.

Even if the material in question qualifies for one of these exemptions, it is still necessary to register the activity which is to be carried out with the Environment Agency. To register, the Agency must be notified of the relevant activities and where they are to be carried out, and the exemption on which it is sought to rely. It is an offence to carry out an exempt activity without registering, and if the activity is not exempt, the person will be in breach of s.33 of the EPA if there has been no application for a WML. In certain circumstances there may also be a requirement for planning permission to cover situations where, for example, waste materials are being re-utilised on site as part of landscaping features, so being exempt from the need for a WML is not entirely without paperwork. It should also be stressed that granting of an exemption is at the discretion of the Environment Agency. There is no right of appeal so, in the event of dissatisfaction with the Agency's decision, the only recourse would be to the judicial review procedure.

5.2.5. Surrender of Waste Management Licences

Once a contract for which a WML is required has been completed, it may not always be possible to terminate the licence. This means that a contractor, or whoever holds the licence, may continue to be responsible for the waste management activities for which he was licensed, long after such activities have ceased.

In the past, before Waste Disposal Licences graduated into WMLs, a licence holder had the right to surrender his licence to the Waste Disposal Authority at any time. This meant that any conditions attached to the licence would automatically cease, enabling the holder to abandon the licensed site and relinquish any future responsibility for it. In this way a person who was technically or financially incompetent to deal with problems which had arisen on the land could simply avoid them. Although any responsibilities which flowed from the planning permission, or which arose out of ownership of the site, if this were the case, could not be ignored, the surrender of the Waste Disposal Licence effectively undermined any attempt to regulate waste disposal sites once operations had ceased.

However, a significant feature of the WML is that the holder is no longer able to surrender a licence unilaterally, but will be subject to the licence conditions until released from them by the Environment Agency on the issue of a certificate of completion. A further, complementary amendment to the old regime is that conditions may be attached to WMLs which will continue to apply after the site has ceased to be used for depositing waste.

Surrender of a WML can only take place if the licence holder applies to the Environment Agency and the Agency accepts the surrender. However, it should be noted that a mobile plant licence covering, for example, equipment which is used for sorting, crushing or grading waste materials, may still be surrendered at will. Before the Agency will accept surrender of a site licence, it must inspect the site and determine whether or not it is likely to cause pollution of the environment or harm to human health. If the Agency considers that the site is likely to cause environmental problems, it must refuse the application to surrender.

An application to surrender a WML must include a considerable amount of information relating to the licence holder and the site, such as

- a detailed description of all activities carried out on the site, whether licensed or not
- the location of those activities
- the period over which they were carried out
- an estimate of the quantity of waste dealt with at the site, and
- where landfill of waste has taken place on site, detailed information relating to matters such as hydrogeology, production of gas and leachate, and the quality of groundwater.

The fact that there is no automatic right to surrender a WML may mean that a contractor, as a licence holder, is left with potential liabilities after the period of the contract has expired. In practice the Environment Agency has been cautious about accepting the surrender of WMLs for fear that it might become liable for any future clean-up costs in the event that there is a waste-related problem with the site. One option which may be available to contractors is the transfer of their WML to the client, or landowner at the end of the contract period. Pursuant to s.40 of the EPA 1990 a WML may be transferred where the holder and the proposed transferee make a joint application to the Environment Agency. The Agency is obliged to make the transfer unless it considers that the proposed transferee is not a 'fit and proper person'. Clearly there may be situations where the client will not be prepared to take over the WML in this way, and if the Environment Agency will not accept its surrender either, the contractor will be left with possible on-going liabilities posed by the site and the waste management activities which have taken place there. Where these potential liabilities are considered to be significant, some form of bespoke insurance might provide a means of off-setting the risk (see further Chapter 8).

5.2.6. The Duty of Care

Section 34 of the EPA 1990 is potentially one of the most far-reaching aspects of the waste management regime, and will be particularly relevant to contractors on site, in that it imposes a criminal Duty of Care on all those who deal with Directive waste. This important duty is intended to ensure that waste is dealt with responsibly from its production to its ultimate disposal. It imposes far greater duties on the producers and intermediate handlers of waste than existed before its introduction on 1 April 1992, and it has necessitated the implementation of effective systems of waste management within all companies which are involved in the waste management chain.

Section 34 applies to any person who 'imports, produces, carries, treats, keeps or disposes of controlled waste, or as a broker, has control of such waste...' and imposes a duty on such people to take reasonable measures to ensure four things

- that no-one else disposes of the waste unlawfully or in a manner likely to cause pollution of the environment or harm to human health
- that it does not escape
- that when the waste is transferred, it is to an authorised person, and
- that a written description of the waste is transferred with it to enable that person to deal with it appropriately.

In practice the Duty means that contractors must

- store and pack waste properly
- describe clearly its constituent elements
- deal only with authorised waste carriers
- provide carriers with an accurate transfer note relating to the waste
- take steps to ensure that it is ultimately disposed of correctly.

There is obviously an element of subjectivity as to what constitutes 'reasonable measures', but guidance is provided in the DoE's revised

Code of Practice on the Duty of Care which contractors should find particularly helpful in clarifying what is expected of them. The Code of Practice is important in that it is admissible in evidence in any prosecution for failing to comply with the Duty of Care and any relevant provision must be taken into account by a court dealing with such a prosecution.

The Duty of Care will normally apply to both contractors and sub-contractors on site, because they will all be generating waste, and the producer of waste is generally regarded as the person undertaking the works, as opposed to the person who issues the instructions or lets contracts which give rise to waste. For this reason, the client will not normally be subject to the Duty of Care. However, where a client or contractor makes arrangements for the carriage or disposal of waste — through a disposal sub-contractor or a haulier, for example — then he will be regarded as a broker of waste and therefore subject to the Duty of Care. Any person who transports waste, even within the boundaries of the site, will also be subject to the Duty.

As everyone in the 'waste chain' is therefore subject to the Duty of Care, there should be an element of self-policing, as well as enforcement by the Environment Agency. This means that in addition to ensuring that waste is stored securely on site, contractors should 'vet' the person to whom they transfer their waste to ensure that they are an 'authorised person'. This will usually mean checking that the carrier to whom waste is given is a registered carrier, or where the person to whom it is being given is responsible for its disposal, that that person is the holder of an appropriate WML.

5.2.7. Transportation of waste

Pursuant to the Control of Pollution (Amendment) Act 1989, supplemented by the Controlled Waste (Registration of Carriers and Seizure of Vehicles) Regulations 1991 (as amended), it is an offence to carry controlled (now 'Directive') waste without being registered with the Environment Agency. In order to comply with the Duty of Care, contractors should check carriers' registrations on a regular basis, even if using a firm which they employ regularly, since registrations can be revoked. Although it will clearly not be necessary to carry out a full check on each transfer, it is recommended that a carrier's registration, or site manager's WML be checked at least once a year. The original or a certified copy should be seen; the Code of Practice advises that a photocopy is not adequate.

Care should also be taken over the written description which is to accompany the waste. This should obviously be full enough to allow the waste to be dealt with appropriately. Furthermore, contractors should be wary of simply passing on to a disposal contractor a description of waste with which they have been furnished, without checking its validity. In addition to the Duty of Care, the Environmental Protection (Duty of Care) Regulations 1991 also impose obligations to document and describe the waste being transferred through the use of a Transfer Note, although it is not actually required to travel with the waste. The Regulations set out all the information to be included in the Transfer Note, such as

- the identity and quantity of the waste
- the nature of its container
- the time and place of transfer, and
- the name, address and other relevant details of the transferor and tranferee.

The written description and the Transfer Note can be combined in one document as long as the requirement for each is met. Both documents must be retained for at least two years from the date of transfer.

Where the waste to be transported is classed as special waste, more stringent rules apply. For further information see Section 5.2.2.

5.2.8. Criminal offences

Where materials are classed as waste and no exemption applies, it is important to remember that a criminal offence is committed when a person keeps, treats or disposes of them other than in accordance with a WML. If a contractor is keeping, treating or disposing of waste on site he should either have an appropriate licence in force or have registered his activities as exempt with the local office of the

Environment Agency. Handling waste without a licence, or in breach of its conditions can lead to prosecution. Similarly a separate offence exists — independent of the licensing regime — where waste is treated, kept or disposed of in a manner likely to cause pollution of the environment or harm to human health. This offence effectively imposes minimum standards as to the way in which waste should be handled. A person found guilty of either of these offences can be sentenced to a fine of up to £20 000 and/or imprisonment for up to six months, if convicted in the Magistrates' Court. On conviction in the Crown Court a person can be imprisoned for up to two years, and/or ordered to pay an unlimited fine. Although in practice imprisonment for waste-related offences is fairly unusual, courts have used their powers in this context for serious offences and where an offender offends repeatedly. However, those convicted of a breach of s.33(1) of the EPA 1990 are more likely to be subject to a fine. An injunction may also be sought by the prosecuting authority in certain cases.

There are three possible defences which are set out at s.33(7) of the EPA 1990 and can be deployed in the following circumstances

- where all reasonable precautions were taken and due diligence exercised to avoid the offence
- where an employee has acted in accordance with instructions from his employer, and there was no reason to suppose that his actions constituted an offence
- where the relevant act took place in an emergency, in order to avoid danger to the public - danger to the *environment* does not constitute a defence in these circumstances - and the Environment Agency was notified of the incident as soon as reasonably practicable.

Breach of the Duty of Care is also a criminal offence. It is important to realise that the Duty is breached irrespective of whether harm is caused — it is the failure to take reasonable measures to comply with it which constitutes the offence. On conviction in the Magistrates' Court, an offender is liable to a fine of up to £5000, or an unlimited fine in the Crown Court.

5.3. THE LANDFILL TAX

5.3.1. The regime

Most material being sent to landfill sites for final disposal, pursuant to a WML, will be subject to the landfill tax, and it is important that contractors consider this liability in tendering for work and allow for the additional costs of waste disposal in pricing any given job.

The landfill tax was introduced in the November 1994 Budget and is outlined in broad terms in the Finance Act 1996, but it also forms the subject of three pieces of secondary legislation.

- The Landfill Tax General Regulations 1996 (SI 1996 No. 1527) cover details of implementation such as registration procedures, tax credits and accounting procedures.
- The Landfill Tax (Qualifying Material) Order 1996 (SI 1996 No. 1528) defines the categories of waste to which the lower rate of tax will apply.
- The Landfill Tax (Contaminated Land) Order 1996 (SI 1996 No. 1529) sets out the exemption provisions in respect of waste cleared from historically-contaminated land.

In addition to raising revenue, the tax is intended to deter the landfilling of waste and encourage recycling. This is in accordance with the UK's European commitment to move more waste up the 'waste management hierarchy'. This hierarchy, in order of preference, consists of waste minimisation, reuse, recovery and final disposal – where incineration is deemed preferable to landfill of waste.

The tax is payable to Customs and Excise by landfill site operators only (with the exception of those who have WMLs to dispose of waste on their own sites) – everyone else pays increased prices for depositing their waste at landfill sites, triggered by the higher overheads to be borne by the site operators. By driving these additional costs back down the waste supply chain, it is hoped that producers of waste will be encouraged to find ways of minimising their waste production and to seek more efficient ways of managing their waste, in accordance with the waste hierarchy.

Waste is taxed by weight, with a distinction being made between active and inactive waste. The current rates of tax (from April 2001) are £12 per tonne for active waste, and £2 per tonne for inactive waste. The rate for active waste is to increase by £1 each year until it reaches £15 per tonne in April 2004, at which point the tax levels are to be re-assessed. The lower rate for inactive waste applies to naturally occurring rocks and soils — including topsoil — ceramic or cemented materials, uncontaminated processed minerals, furnace slags, ashes, certain low-activity inorganic compounds and gypsum and plaster materials. Mixtures consisting of these wastes alone qualify for the lower rate, as does water with suspended solids consisting only of these wastes.

The construction industry has been highly critical of the two-tiered approach to the tax on account of the fact that it disposes of large quantities of relatively harmless, low-value waste, such as rubble, wood and plastics, most of which, however, is liable for tax at the higher rate. Another issue which is particularly pertinent to the construction industry is the permissible level of contamination of inactive wastes by active ingredients before waste attracts the higher rate of tax. Where overwhelmingly inactive loads contain incidental amounts of active waste, such as a load of concrete waste for example, which contains a small piece of wood, a certain amount of leeway is permitted and the load can be taxed as 'inactive waste'. Where large quantities of predominantly inert materials are collected for disposal from construction sites, contractors may find it cost-effective to implement a system to sort the waste on site, although this may prove an unrealistic aim on sites where skips tend to acquire discarded sofas and white goods over the weekend ... .

Landfill operators have adopted a variety of approaches for calculating the price increase to be passed on to their customers. Some operators have chosen to adopt a fixed-price increase per tonne, to cover all loads of waste, thereby avoiding individual negotiations with each customer. However, operators are still required to be aware of the contents of all in-coming waste, both to comply with the Duty of Care under s.34 of the EPA 1990, and so as to be able to account accurately for the amount of tax payable to Customs and Excise.

5.3.2. Exemptions from the landfill tax

Although most waste disposed of to landfill will be subject to the tax, there are a few important exemptions from the regime including

- dredgings
- most mine and quarry waste, and
- waste removed from historically-contaminated sites during reclamation, but not development, of a site.

Waste generated by a reclamation project qualifies for exemption if the reclamation project is carried out to facilitate

- development
- conservation
- the provision of a public park or other amenity, or
- the use of the land for agriculture or forestry.

Alternatively, if it is carried out to reduce or remove the potential of pollutants to cause harm, waste generated by the project will also qualify, but there are a number of conditions which must be met

- the reclamation must constitute or include the removal of pollutants which are causing harm or have the potential to cause harm
- the pollutants must be such that, unless cleared, they would prevent the object concerned (e.g. the development) from going ahead, and
- the activities which gave rise to the pollutants must have ceased.

If it is thought that a project will meet the criteria set out above, an application should be made to Customs and Excise for an Exemption Certificate which will cover the disposal of material from the site during the period of reclamation. In the case of building or civil engineering works, this period will expire when construction commences, or when pollutants have been cleared to the extent that they no longer prevent the development from going ahead, or the potential for harm has been removed. In other words, the Exemption Certificate will be set to expire once the initial site clearance or excavation works are complete — it will not cover disposal of waste generated from the construction phases of the project.

The Exemption Certificate may be subject to conditions such as, it will relate only to a particular quantity of material, it may only relate to disposals made at specified sites, or it may relate to material from only one part of the site. It may subsequently be varied, or a new Certificate issued where necessary.

The person intending to carry out the reclamation work must apply in writing to Customs and Excise at least 30 days before the relevant disposal of waste to landfill is due to start. An application form must be completed and returned to Customs and Excise, together with the following, where possible

- site plans, independent surveys and planning permission — if appropriate
- a chemist's reports on the nature and level of pollution
- an independent survey of the area and depth of contamination, with an estimate of the total weight of waste from the certified area to be disposed of to landfill
- copies of any contracts or surveys relating to the reclamation
- name and address of the landfill site(s) to which the waste will be taken, with details of the weight and type of waste to be sent to each site, and
- the dates between which the disposals will take place.

It is the responsibility of the person reclaiming the land to apply for an Exemption Certificate, and that person must be in possession of the Certificate before landfilling the contaminated waste, as otherwise the waste is taxable. Customs and Excise are not permitted to backdate Certificates, so it is important to comply with the 30-day application period. It is possible to have a Certificate varied in certain circumstances

- where further pollutants are discovered
- where there are other changes to the tonnage to be landfilled, or
- where the landfill site to be used has changed.

If a reclamation scheme has the potential to qualify for an exemption, it is worth making the application to Customs and Excise sooner rather than later, with a view to getting the Certificate varied should the reclamation project unearth any surprises. An amendment to a Certificate will usually be processed within five working days of

Customs and Excise's receipt of notification.

On completion of the reclamation works, a completion statement must be sent to Customs and Excise summarising, by reference to each landfill use

- the start and finish dates of the qualifying disposals, and
- the total tonnage disposed of.

5.4 SUMMARY

The definition of 'waste' and what constitutes waste 'disposal' is a very complex area of law. The nature of the construction process is such that opportunities will regularly arise where it is possible to incorporate materials which may or may not be regarded as 'waste' into the development design, thereby minimising waste disposal and landfill tax costs. Even where such materials are not classed as waste for the purposes of the waste management regime, or are covered by an exemption, they need to be handled with care, as they may have the potential to cause ground and surface water pollution, contaminate the soil or lead to unacceptable emissions to the atmosphere. The flow chart shown at Figure 1 is intended to provide a guide through the law in this area, but before assuming that material which is to be recycled on site is not 'waste', legal advice should be sought.

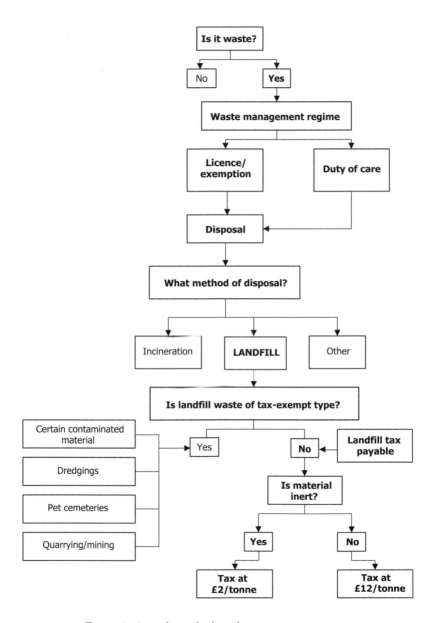

Figure 1. A guide to the law for waste management

6

Water pollution

6.1. INTRODUCTION

The Environment Agency has general responsibility for management of water resources and protection of the aquatic environment pursuant to the Water Resources Act 1991. The regulatory system involves the setting of water quality objectives for inland, coastal, estuarial and ground waters; a requirement that a discharge consent is obtained from the Environment Agency for discharges of trade or sewage effluent to these waters; and a requirement that a licence is obtained from the Agency where abstractions are to be made. The WRA 1991 also creates a number of criminal offences in respect of pollution of these waters. This Chapter will first discuss how to apply for a discharge consent or abstraction licence, before explaining the criminal offences which may be committed as a result of a water pollution incident.

Statistics compiled from Environment Agency data show that the construction industry is amongst the most frequently prosecuted industries for water pollution offences. There are probably a number of reasons for this. A risk to watercourses will arise where construction work is carried out adjacent to rivers and streams, or in the vicinity of beaches or estuaries, or where underground streams and aquifers exist close to the works. Construction sites are home to a number of hazardous substances – as will be discussed further in Chapter 7 –

and, in addition, more apparently benign substances such as uncontaminated soil can prove a persistent and aggressive pollutant when flushed into water. Traditional construction processes such as piling, drilling and excavating, which disturb the subsoil, can cause pollutants in the ground to migrate to watercourses. When viewed in the context of 'strict liability' which has traditionally been the legislature's approach to water pollution offences (see Section 1.3.1), it is perhaps not surprising that the construction industry does not have a very good record in relation to water pollution.

6.2. DISCHARGES INTO CONTROLLED WATERS

6.2.1. Water discharge consents

Where a contractor is aware that a construction project is going to involve making a discharge to 'controlled waters', or require abstraction of water from a local watercourse, it will generally be advisable to make the necessary licence applications in advance of starting work on site, because of the time delay which a licence application can entail.

The definition of 'controlled waters' can be found at s.104 of the WRA 1991 and includes virtually all inland, ground and coastal waters. Controlled waters consist of four sub-categories

- relevant territorial waters, i.e. the sea within a line three miles out from the baselines from which the territorial sea is measured
- coastal waters, i.e. the sea within those baselines up to the line of the highest tide, and tidal waters up to the fresh water limit as defined by the Secretary of State
- inland waters, i.e. rivers, streams, underground streams, canals, lakes and reservoirs – including those which are temporarily dry, and
- groundwaters, i.e. any waters contained in underground strata or in wells or boreholes.

The only waters which are generally excluded are landlocked waters which do not drain into other controlled waters, although the

Secretary of State has the power to include or exclude specific waters by order. Water supply mains and pipes, and sewers and drains – where separate controls on discharges apply (see Section 6.4 below) – are also excluded from the definition of controlled waters.

There has also been some further clarification by the courts who have held that a river bed can form part of 'controlled waters' (*NRA v. Biffa Waste*), as can a man-made ditch if it drains into controlled waters (*Environment Agency v. Brock plc*).

As to the meaning of 'discharge', a matter of particular concern and uncertainty is run-off and a brief digression is warranted. This will also help to distinguish consents for discharges into controlled waters from those for discharges into surface water drains or foul sewers. Virtually every construction site, regardless of its proximity to controlled waters, will be subject to rainwater run-off, although the regulatory position as regards related discharge consents will vary according to the nature of the site.

- Where run-off consists of uncontaminated rain water, no form of discharge consent is required. Other run-off, whether discharged in a controlled fashion or simply the natural product of the situation, will generally require a consent or amount to the commission of an offence.
- Where run-off is contaminated with soil, for example, and it is being discharged into controlled waters, a discharge consent will usually be required from the Environment Agency.
- In circumstances where contaminated run-off is discharged into a surface water drain, this may be vested in the local sewerage undertaker, in which case a discharge consent should be sought from the latter rather than the Environment Agency (because controlled waters are not involved). See Section 6.4 for details. The drainage department of the local authority should be able to supply the necessary information as to who should be approached regarding any particular discharge, and if in doubt, it would be prudent to consult the Environment Agency.
- Where run-off is polluted with potentially-hazardous substances – from a contaminated site, for example – it will usually be necessary to discharge it to a foul water sewer, which will require a trade

effluent consent from the local sewerage undertaker. See Section 6.4 for further details. Such sites may require wheel-washing facilities for all vehicles which use the site to minimise the spread of contamination within the site, and to prevent off-site contamination. Water used for wheel-washing on a contaminated site containing heavy metals, for example, would usually be discharged to a sewer, in accordance with a trade effluent consent.

A separate consent is required for each discharge to controlled waters, and applications should be made to the Environment Agency. Although the Agency has a discretion as to what information it requires in respect of the proposed discharge, the applicant should generally state the place, nature, quantity, rate of flow, composition and temperature of the proposed discharge. Having received the application, there are a number of steps which must be completed by the Agency.

- The Agency must publicise the application in a local newspaper and in the *London Gazette*, and notify any relevant local authorities and water undertakers, at the applicant's expense.
- The Agency must take into account any written representations made within six weeks of the notice being advertised.
- Where the Agency intends to grant the consent it must inform anyone who made written representations of this fact and then wait a further 21 days.

The Agency has the power to grant the consent either conditionally or unconditionally, or to refuse it. A fee is payable to the Agency for making an application for a new or revised consent, and in addition there are annual charges made for all discharge consents. Details of the current rates are available from the local regional office of the Environment Agency.

The Environment Agency may impose 'such conditions as it thinks fit', but conditions generally relate to the following in respect of the discharge

- quality
- quantity
- nature

- composition
- temperature
- the siting and design of the outlet
- monitoring and sampling requirements, and
- information to be provided to the Agency.

The Agency has a duty to review consents from time to time, and a variation or revocation can be made simply by notifying the discharger.

An application is deemed to have been refused if no decision is given within four months. The applicant has the right to appeal to the Secretary of State if the Environment Agency refuses the permission sought, or imposes conditions which are felt to be unacceptable. However, where the applicant is not satisfied with the conditions imposed by a consent, or the consent has been refused outright, it may be worth trying to negotiate an acceptable form of consent with the Environment Agency before launching an appeal.

6.2.2. Criminal offences

The principal water pollution offences are contained within s.85 of the WRA 1991. Subject to certain defences, a person will commit an offence if he causes or knowingly permits

- any poisonous, noxious or polluting matter or any solid matter to enter any controlled waters
- any matter, other than trade effluent or sewage effluent, to enter controlled waters by being discharged from a drain or a sewer in contravention of a relevant prohibition
- any trade effluent or sewage effluent to be discharged
  (i)   into any controlled waters, or
  (ii) from land in England and Wales to a pipe into the sea outside the seaward limits of controlled waters
- any trade effluent or sewage effluent to be discharged from a building or from any fixed plant on to or into any land or into a lake or pond which does not discharge directly or indirectly into a river or watercourse (i.e. not a discharge to controlled waters) where the Environment Agency has specifically prohibited such discharge, or

- any matter whatever to enter any inland waters so as to tend (either directly or indirectly or in combination with other matter which he or another person permits to enter those waters) to impede the proper flow of the waters in a manner leading or likely to lead to a substantial aggravation of
  (i)   pollution due to other causes, or
  (ii) the consequences of such pollution.

Water pollution offences, like most environmental offences, are what is known as 'triable either way' which means that they may be heard in the Magistrates' Court or the Crown Court, depending on the severity of the offence which has been committed. On conviction in the Magistrates' Court there is a maximum fine of £20 000 and/or three months in prison. On conviction in the Crown Court there can be an unlimited fine, and/or a two-year prison sentence. For a first offence, where there has been no harm to fish and remediation has been relatively straightforward and inexpensive, a defendant might anticipate a fine in the region of £2000 to £5000, with costs for the Environment Agency in the region of £500 to £1000. The Court is likely to adopt a more tolerant view towards the defendant company where every effort has been made to co-operate with the Agency, and clean-up costs have been paid without dispute. For a second or subsequent offence, or where the evidence suggests negligence or reckless disregard for the aquatic environment, the fine can range between £5000 and £20 000. Fines in excess of £20 000 are relatively rare, even though the Crown Court has the power to impose unlimited fines.

The Environment Agency has a discretion to prosecute, and not every breach of water pollution legislation will result in prosecution of the perpetrator. The Agency's response to a pollution incident should be governed by its *Enforcement and Prosecution Policy*, and its internal guidelines which relate to specific offences and breaches. The so-called 'Functional Guidelines' set out the Common Incident Classsification Scheme (CICS) which is a national system for categorising pollution incidents and assessing the appropriate level of enforcement response. A brief summary of these documents is set out at Section 1.4.1. However, the health warning as regards this categorisation is, of course, that it can at best be regarded as a rule of thumb and, however closely this sort of approach is promoted by the Agency, there will always be scope for exceptions and deviations.

6.2.3. Defences

There are a number of defences which are provided by the WRA 1991 in ss. 88 and 89.

If the entry or discharge in question is caused or permitted in an emergency in order to avoid danger to life or death, the person responsible takes all such steps as are reasonably practicable in the circumstances for minimising the extent of the entry or discharge and of its polluting effects, and particulars of the entry or discharge are furnished to the Environment Agency as soon as reasonably practicable after it occurs, then this would constitute a defence.

If the entry or discharge in question complied with a discharge consent issued by the Environment Agency, then this would also be a defence. The function of the licence, permit, authorisation or consent is to make lawful that which would otherwise be unlawful. An activity carried out in accordance with such a permission will not be a criminal offence. Normally, an offence will be committed if the appropriate type of permission is not obtained. Application for an appropriate discharge consent is dealt with at Section 6.2.1.

It is important to realise, however, that a licence, permit, authorisation or consent granted by an enforcing authority will not provide a defence to civil proceedings brought by a person whose private rights have been infringed. This means that a consent granted by the Environment Agency to discharge trade effluent into a river will not prevent a downstream landowner from bringing an action against the person to whom the consent has been granted in respect of the deterioration in quality of the river water flowing through his land. For further information about liability in tort, see Section 1.3.2.2.

6.2.4. 'Cause or knowingly permit'

As can be seen from Section 6.2.2 above, the legislation covering the control of polluting discharges to water, hinges on the interpretation of 'cause or knowingly permit'. There is now a considerable body of case-law which assists in the interpretation of these words. The phrase creates two separate offences, one 'causing', the other 'knowingly permitting'. The offence of *causing* pollution is clearly a strict liability offence, in that it does not require the prosecution to prove that the defendant committed the offence with knowledge, merely that he committed it. Therefore the defendant does not need to have been negligent in any way to be convicted.

The leading case on 'causing' pollution in this context is the House of Lords' decision in *Alphacell Limited v. Woodward*. The defendants prepared manilla fibres during their paper-manufacturing process, and water used to wash the fibres was pumped into settling tanks. Pumps had been installed which were designed to switch off automatically when water in the tanks reached a certain level. The objective was to prevent the tanks from overflowing into a river. However, the pumps were obstructed by fern and leaves and consequently failed to operate correctly. Polluted water from the tanks overflowed into the river. The defendants were convicted of causing polluting matter to enter a river contrary to s.2(1) of the Rivers (Prevention of Pollution) Act 1951 which is a predecessor to the s.85 'poisonous, noxious and polluting matter' offence under the WRA 1991. The defendants appealed ultimately to the House of Lords, but the House upheld the conviction, holding that it was not necessary to prove that the defendants acted with knowledge, intent or out of neglect. It was sufficient that they had set the process in motion and therefore caused the pollution in question. In the words of Lord Wilberforce:

> 'The whole complex operation which might lead to this result was an operation deliberately conducted by the [defendants] and I fail to see how a defect in one stage of it, even if we assume that this happened without negligence, can enable them to say that they did not cause the pollution.'

The consequence of this decision is clearly very important in that it means that where a person causes any polluting matter to enter controlled waters, the fact that the discharge was not intended, and the person was in no way negligent in allowing it to happen, will not save him from conviction.

However, the chain of causation may be considered to have been broken in two situations

- three Law Lords in *Alphacell Limited v. Woodward* suggested that the defence of Act of God may be applicable to sever the causal connection. An example might be pollution caused by freak or unforeseeable weather conditions
- the chain of causation may be broken by the intervention of a third party.

This occurred in *Impress (Worcester) Limited v. Rees*, where a trespasser opened a valve in an oil storage tank belonging to the defendant, releasing oil which then flowed into a river. However, in a more recent House of Lords case, *Empress Car Company v. NRA* it was decided that the *Impress* decision was wrong, and that where the pollution resulted from the 'ordinary' — which appears to mean, foreseeable — actions of a third party, this did not change the fact that it had ultimately been *caused* by the defendants.

In *Empress Car Company v. NRA*, the defendant company had kept diesel in an unbunded tank governed by a tap with no lock, in a yard which drained directly into a river. An unknown person opened the tap and the entire contents of the tank overflowed and passed by way of a drain into the river. The facts of this case were similar to those in the *Impress* case, but the Lords held that the fact that someone or something else caused the pollution was not inconsistent with the defendant having caused it. The prosecution did not need to show that the defendant did something which was the immediate cause of the pollution; maintaining tanks of noxious liquid was 'doing something', even if the immediate cause of the pollution was lack of maintenance, a natural event or the act of a third party.

It can therefore be seen that only extraordinary interventions by a third party are likely to be sufficient to break the causal chain; it is a matter of degree.

Contractors should therefore take particular care to secure their sites so as to prevent acts of vandalism or trespass by third parties, because on the basis of the *Empress Car Company* decision these may be classed as 'ordinary' events, and as such insufficient to break the causal link between the contractor and any resulting pollution incidents.

A poorly-secured site might also put a contractor in a position of having 'knowingly permitted' pollution – which is the second offence created by s.85 of the WRA 1991 – if it was felt that inadequate steps had been taken to avoid the occurrence of the pollution event. The second limb of the s.85 offence – 'knowingly permitting' pollution – has tended to cause fewer problems of interpretation than the primary offence, and is generally construed to mean a failure to prevent pollution, where the defendant had knowledge of the pollution.

6.3. ANTI-POLLUTION WORKS

Under ss.161 and 161A–D of the WRA 1991 (introduced by Schedule 22 of the Environmental Act 1995), and brought into force in March 1999 by the Anti-Pollution Works Regulations 1999, the Environment Agency has widely-drafted powers to take action, or require action to be taken by others, in cases where any poisonous, noxious or polluting matter, or any solid waste, is likely to enter controlled waters or is present or has been present in those waters. The power to carry out anti-pollution works may only be exercised following service of a works notice on the appropriate responsible person, as defined in s.161B, unless it is necessary to carry out the works 'forthwith'.

If it carries out works itself, the Environment Agency can recover the costs incurred in these works, operations or investigations from anyone who has caused or knowingly permitted the pollutant to be present in, or a threat to, controlled waters.

The 1999 Regulations give the Environment Agency specific powers

- to serve works notices on the person/company managing the site specifying works or operations required to be carried out once a pollution incident has occurred

- to serve a works notice to prevent a potential pollution incident
- to require the restoration of waters – and any dependent flora and fauna – to their state immediately before polluting matter entered them, and
- to recover the costs of any investigations needed to determine the source of pollution from the persons on whom notices are served.

Failure to comply with a works notice is a criminal offence which, if proved may result in imprisonment, a fine or both. If a works notice is not complied with, the Environment Agency may come onto the land and carry out the works stipulated in the notice and recover its costs for expenses reasonably incurred. If the Environment Agency takes this action it could result in contractors having to down tools while the work is implemented resulting in slippage in building programmes.

It is possible to appeal against the work specified by a works notice but there are strict time limits in which to lodge any appeal. Notices will not be suspended pending the outcome of an appeal.

The emphasis of the Regulations is on the implementation of measures to prevent water pollution or potential water pollution. As a works notice can be served where the Agency thinks that there is *potential* for a pollution incident, all those responsible for managing construction sites should give careful thought to implementing practical measures to prevent water pollution on- and off-site (silt and oil are probably the substances most likely to give rise to water pollution incidents on construction sites) to avoid service of works notices.

These powers may also be applicable in circumstances where the statutory framework for contaminated land remediation (see Section 4.2) does not allow a determination that land is 'contaminated' because substances have already entered controlled waters. According to the statutory guidance, where a substance is already dissolved, or in suspension, in controlled waters, it should be deemed to have entered controlled waters and therefore be unable to cause any further pollution. The s.78 EPA 1990 clean-up regime cannot therefore be triggered in such circumstances. However, it is intended that the WRA 1991 anti-pollution works provisions are broadly consistent with the new contaminated land regime where pollution of controlled waters, or the threat of pollution is involved, hence the amendments introduced by Schedule 22 of the Environment Act 1995, and implemented by the 1999 Regulations.

6.4. DISPOSAL OF WASTE TO SEWERS

Private water and sewerage undertakers provide the public water supply and own and operate the sewerage network and sewage works. They are also responsible for regulating discharges to sewers. The regulatory regime covering discharges to sewers is contained within the Water Industry Act 1991, and is based on a system of individualised consents set by the operators of the sewers.

It is a criminal offence to discharge any trade effluent from trade premises into sewers without a trade effluent consent. Trade effluent is defined in s.141(1) of the WIA 1991 to mean

- any liquid, either with or without particles of matter in suspension in the liquid, which is wholly or partly produced in the course of any trade or industry carried out at trade premises, and
- in relation to any trade premises, any such liquid which is so produced in the course of any trade or industry carried on at those premises.

Trade premises are defined as any premises used or intended to be used for carrying on any trade or industry.

The discharger applies for a trade effluent consent by serving notice on the sewerage undertaker at least two months prior to starting to discharge. In order that the sewerage undertaker can gauge the likely impact of the discharge, the notice must state

- the nature and composition of the proposed effluent
- the maximum daily volume, and
- the maximum rate of discharge.

The sewerage undertaker has a discretion whether to grant the consent, but where the sewerage system can cope with the discharge, a consent is normally given subject to conditions. Section 121 of the WIA 1991 sets out the scope of conditions which may be set with reference to a list of matters such as

- the time and place of the discharge
- the nature, temperature and pH of the discharge
- the provision, testing and maintenance of sampling equipment
- monitoring requirements, and
- record-keeping.

The sewerage undertaker has the power to vary a consent unilaterally provided that the discharger is given two months' notice, although variation of a consent is only possible after two years have elapsed following the initial consent or a previous variation. The discharger has the right to appeal to the Director General of OFWAT against refusal or variation of the consent, or on the basis of conditions imposed. However, there is no right of appeal against the trade effluent charges which are levied by the sewerage undertakers. These charges are calculated on the basis of the volume and strength of the discharge and it is therefore advisable for dischargers to consider whether their trade effluent discharges can be minimised so as to reduce costs, as well as to minimise waste.

The penalty for the offence of discharging without a consent, or in breach of a condition, is punishable by a fine of up to £5000 on conviction in the Magistrates' Court, and in the Crown Court the fine is unlimited. The sewerage undertakers are responsible for enforcing the regime. Although their approach to enforcement tends to be conciliatory rather than aggressive, their own obligations in respect of Environment Agency consents for treatment plants which discharge to controlled waters, mean that they are keen to ensure that nothing enters the sewerage system which might cause them to be in breach.

7

Site hazards and nuisances

7.1. INTRODUCTION

Once work starts on site, there is considerable scope for various types of environmental liabilities to attach to contractors, whether as a result of existing problems on site (such as contaminated soil), or of new problems created by the contractor (such as pollution of a nearby watercourse), in addition to any contractual liabilities which may arise. This Chapter will look at the various risks which contractors should consider before work commences on site in order that they can take steps, where possible, to minimise any environmental impact and avoid confrontation with the regulators, the risk of prosecution, criminal fines, actions for damages, injunctions – which could result in delay to the project – and occasionally even, imprisonment.

7.2. SITE HAZARDS

7.2.1. Dangers to the environment

Each construction site will have its own particular hazards, but there are a number of common ones of which contractors should be aware, in order to avoid breaching environmental or health and safety legislation.

- Consideration should be given to the potential to pollute water, either surface water or underground sources. If there are known sources or accumulations of water in close proximity to the site, particular care should be taken with substances which are to be used on site which have the potential to pollute water or soil if they should escape.
- Although the employer may have certain contractual responsibilities to inform the contractor of local conditions, such as the identification of contaminated land, it would be prudent for the contractor to conduct his own preliminary survey to identify the potential effects of the project on the surrounding environment and his workforce.
- Particular attention should be given to the fact that many of the potential hazards lie underground, making them additionally vulnerable to being overlooked.
- Underground watercourses, sewers, pipelines and cables can all present problems if only discovered by chance during excavation works. The water industry, for example, depends on the proper functioning of an extensive network of pressure pipelines, representing a large financial investment. Damage or disruption to customer supplies may prove a costly mistake for a contractor in itself, but where a damaged water main, for example, leads to flooding of the works, or pollution of a nearby watercourse, the implications can be more far-reaching.
- Even where a soil survey has been carried out to identify the presence of hazardous substances on site, the contractor should be aware that isolated pockets of contamination may have been overlooked.
- In addition to hazardous substances contained within the soil, there may be materials, such as asbestos, used in the fabric of existing buildings, or brought on site for incorporation into the new development, which pose a threat to both the workforce and the environment.

The principal regulatory implications of a contaminated site, waste management on site and water pollution have all been discussed in some detail in Chapters 4, 5 and 6 respectively. However, as many of the potential hazards on a construction site pose a threat to the workforce as well as to the environment, contractors also need to consider the safety and well-being of their employees and sub-contractors.

7.2.2. Dangers to visitors

In addition, contractors should be aware that they also owe a duty of care to visitors and trespassers on their sites, under the Occupiers' Liability Acts of 1957 (lawful visitors) and 1984 (unlawful visitors, ie. trespassers). The duty owed to a visitor is defined by s.2(2) of the 1957 Act, which imposes upon an occupier

'A duty to take such care as in all the circumstances is reasonable
to see that the visitor will be reasonably safe in using the premises
for the purposes for which he is invited or permitted by the occupier
to be there.'

The duty to a trespasser is limited in s.1(4) of the Occupiers' Liability Act 1984 to

'the duty...to take such care as is reasonable in all the
circumstances of the case to see that he does not suffer injury on
the premises by reason of the danger concerned'

and only arises, under s.1(3) of that Act, where

- the occupier knows of the danger or has constructive knowledge of it (i.e. where he *ought* to know)
- the occupier knows, or has constructive knowledge, that the trespasser is in the vicinity or may come into the vicinity of the danger, and
- the danger is one which, in all the circumstances, the occupier can reasonably be expected to offer protection against.

Children are the obvious trespassing hazard which contractors need to guard against. Construction sites hold considerable attraction for children old enough to find a way in, who may not be old enough to appreciate the dangers, and contractors need to ensure that they have taken adequate measures to secure site perimeters and that within the perimeter potential hazards are securely stored or enclosed, as appropriate. Contrary to what is often believed to be the case, the fact that someone is a trespasser does not mean he or she must look out for himself or herself.

7.2.3. Dangers to employees

Where there is a risk of hazardous substances being present on site, contractors must ensure that their employees are adequately trained and equipped to deal with such substances, pursuant to the Control of Substances Hazardous to Health Regulations 1999 and their subsequent amendments (COSHH Regulations). Potential problems are indicated by the discovery during excavation of things such as

- drums, cylinders, storage tanks or other receptacles which might have contained, or still contain, hazardous substances
- unexpected 'soft spots'
- sudden ingress of discoloured or odorous liquid
- excavated material of unusual colour or texture.

In addition to potentially-hazardous materials which are discovered on site, contractors tend to introduce to the site a range of products used in the construction process which have the potential to cause harm if not handled appropriately. Such substances include paints, solvents, cement, plaster, and asbestos, as well as lubricants and fuels used for plant and machinery — any of which can be harmful to personnel and the environment, in certain circumstances. Those substances which are specifically defined as hazardous create certain obligations for contractors in respect of their employees. The COSHH Regulations define 'substance hazardous to health' as any substance which is any of the following

- a substance listed in the Approved Supply List of dangerous substances appended to the Chemicals (Hazard Information and Packaging for Supply) Regulations 1994 (the CHIP Regulations) and is classed therein as very toxic, toxic, harmful, corrosive, irritant etc. The List is regularly amended and an up-to-date version is available on-line through a searchable database at www.the-ncec.com/cselite.

There is a link to this site from the Health and Safety Executive's website which has several pages on the CHIP Regulations at www.hse.gov.uk/hthdir/noframes/chip/chip1/htm

- a substance for which the Health and Safety Commission has approved a maximum exposure limit or an occupational exposure standard
- a biological agent
- a substantial concentration of airborne dust, or
- any other substance that creates a comparable health hazard.

Where hazardous substances exist on site, the COSHH Regulations impose certain duties on contractors — and employers in general — which are intended to minimise the risk posed by such substances to employees. These obligations include

- an assessment of operations, conducted as often as is necessary, to determine any risk of injury from exposure to hazardous substances
- prevention or minimisation of the likelihood of such exposure, so far as reasonably practicable
- ensuring the proper use, maintenance and repair of all control measures and systems, so far as reasonably practicable
- provision of adequate monitoring and health surveillance for any employees who may be exposed to hazardous substances, so far as reasonably practicable, and
- provision of information, instruction and training to anyone who may be exposed to hazardous substances.

If it is not reasonably practicable for a contractor to limit the risk of exposure to hazardous substances by direct means, such as through complete enclosure of that substance, he may provide suitable personal protective equipment (PPE) as a means of risk reduction. However, PPE is always to be considered the method of last resort when reducing the risk of injury. The Personal Protective Equipment at Work Regulations 1992 have a wide application and define 'personal protective equipment' to mean 'all equipment (including clothing affording protection against the weather) which is intended to be worn or held by a person at work and which protects him against one or more risks to his health and safety, and any addition or accessory designed to meet that objective'. Employers must assess the need for PPE and provide it in circumstances where hazardous substances on site necessitate its use. PPE should be suitable for the task and the wearer, and should be properly stored and maintained. Employers also have a duty to ensure that operatives required to wear PPE are given appropriate training in its proper use.

In summary, while health and safety on construction sites is outside the scope of this book, contractors should be aware of the need to control hazardous substances on site to protect both their workforce and the environment. There are a number of publications on the subject of construction site health and safety, including *Masons' Guide: Health and Safety Law for the Construction Industry*. In respect of other hazards, contractors are recommended to carry out a general preliminary survey of the site, and to make enquiries of the relevant authorities to provide an overview from which to assess the potential risks the site may pose.

7.3. STATUTORY NUISANCE

7.3.1. *The offence of statutory nuisance*

The common law concept of nuisance is dealt with in general terms in Chapter 1. Nuisance is generally defined as the unlawful interference by one person with another's use or enjoyment of his land. The use or condition of the land which constitutes the nuisance must generally be unreasonable, and must be fairly persistent; in other words a few hours of piling or drilling one afternoon, causing noise, vibration and dust — however annoying to neighbouring landowners — is unlikely to give rise to a successful claim in nuisance because the interference is transient in nature. Chapter 1 has explained how the common law only offers a partial remedy to problems of an environmental nature, and for this reason the law of statutory nuisance was introduced to provide a bridge between the common-law controls of environmental protection and the more characteristic statutory mechanisms.

In relation to noise, dust and odour, which are probably the most common forms of nuisance caused by the construction industry, the common law is supplemented by Part III of the EPA 1990 which creates the concept of 'statutory nuisance'. Statutory nuisance has a long history, having developed from a public health mechanism into a quick and easy method to abate nuisances, and it is regularly used to combat environmental concerns such as noise, dust and odour.

Pursuant to s.79 of the EPA 1990, local authorities are under a duty to inspect their areas from time to time, to detect statutory nuisances and, perhaps surprisingly, to take enforcement action when they detect or anticipate a nuisance being caused. The fact that a public body is responsible for enforcement should mean that statutory nuisance represents more of a threat than does a common-law action which usually requires the plaintiff to foot the cost of enforcement itself.

7.3.2. Types of statutory nuisance

Matters which might give rise to statutory nuisance under the EPA 1990 are defined in somewhat unhelpful language at s.79(1) and include

- premises in such a state as to be prejudicial to health or a nuisance
- smoke, fumes or gases emitted from premises so as to be prejudicial to health or a nuisance
- dust, steam, smell or other effluvia arising on industrial, trade or business premises and being prejudicial to health or a nuisance
- any accumulation or deposit which is prejudicial to health or a nuisance
- noise emitted from premises so as to be prejudicial to health or a nuisance, or
- noise emitted from or caused by a vehicle, machinery or equipment in a street that is prejudicial to health or a nuisance.

This final point was introduced by the Noise and Statutory Nuisance Act 1993 to extend the scope of the statutory nuisance regime. It reinforces local authorities' powers and enables them to take action against noise in the street. This includes noise from vehicles, equipment, machinery or loudspeakers, and could be relevant in the context of construction site noise. It does not apply to noise made by traffic (see s.79[(6A)] of the EPA 1990). Also, note that a claim of statutory nuisance is not available where a notice has been served under s.60 of the Control of Pollution Act 1974 (see below) or an agreement under s. 61 of that Act is in place and, in each case, is being complied with.

'Prejudicial to health' is defined at s.79(7) of the EPA 1990 as meaning injurious, or likely to cause injury, to health. The word 'nuisance' is generally regarded as having the same meaning as that under the common law, which means that its meaning is somewhat vague. Given the wide range of possible nuisances, in addition to noise, dust and odour, s.79 could previously be used in the context of a contaminated site where the condition of the land gave rise to pollution of water or constituted a dangerous deposit. However, having formulated a regime as complex as the new legal framework for contaminated land − introduced by the Environment Act 1995 and described in detail in Chapter 4 − the Government felt that it would be inappropriate to allow the less precisely-defined system of statutory nuisance to remain as an alternative. The statutory nuisance provisions in Part III of the EPA 1990 have therefore been amended so that they will no longer apply to a statutory nuisance which is created by land being in a 'contaminated state': see s.79[(1A)].

7.3.3. Enforcement procedure

Section 80 of the EPA 1990 provides that where a local authority is satisfied that a statutory nuisance exists, or is likely to occur or recur, it is under a duty to serve an abatement notice on the person responsible for the nuisance, or, if that person cannot be found, on the owner or occupier of the site from which the statutory nuisance emanates. A statutory nuisance differs from the tort of nuisance in that there is no requirement for the notice to be supported by evidence that a particular neighbour has suffered unreasonable intereference with the enjoyment of his property. However, the wording of the notice must be clear and precise as to what must be done to comply and by when, because non-compliance with the terms of the notice can lead to criminal sanctions.

Section 81(5) of the EPA 1990 permits a local authority to take action in the High Court to secure the abatement or restriction of a statutory nuisance, where it feels that proceedings for an offence of contravening an abatement notice would not provide a sufficient remedy.

The offence is only triable in the Magistrates' Court and if found guilty a private offender can be fined up to £5000, with a further fine of up to £500 a day, for each day the offence continues after conviction. A trade or business offender is liable for a fine of up to £20 000. Magistrates also have discretion to award compensation of up to £5000 for contravention of an abatement notice. However, although compensation payments under criminal law are payable, leading commentators Bell and McGillivray suggest that they are rarely ordered (see p. 441 *Ball and Bell on Environmental Law*, 5th Edition, 2000).

The person served with the notice can appeal to the Magistrates' Court within 21 days from the day on which he was served with it. The Statutory Nuisance (Appeals) Regulations 1995 set out the grounds of appeal against an abatement notice, which include

- that the abatement notice is not justified in terms of s.80
- that there has been a substantive or procedural error in the service of the notice
- that the authority has unreasonably refused to accept compliance with alternative requirements, or that its requirements are unreasonable or unnecessary
- that the period for compliance is unreasonable, or
- that the best practicable means were used to avert a nuisance from trade or business premises.

These Regulations also allow the notice to be suspended pending the court's decision, unless the local authority overrides the suspension on the basis that

- the nuisance is prejudicial to health, or
- suspension would render the notice of no practical effect — for example, where the nuisance would have ceased by the time the

action came to court, or

- any expenditure incurred before an appeal would be disproportionate to the public benefit.

On account of the fact that environmental health departments are often overworked and under-resourced, the statutory nuisance provisions do not tend to be used in the proactive way suggested by s.79(1) of the EPA 1990, which imposes a duty on local authorities to inspect their areas from time to time to detect statutory nuisances. In practice what more often happens is that aggrieved individuals notify the local authority about potential problems. If an individual complains of a statutory nuisance emanating from within a given local authority's area, that authority has a duty to take such steps as are reasonably practicable to investigate.

Where the local authority is not inclined to act, s.82 of the EPA 1990 allows a complaint to be made to the local Magistrates' Court by any person who is aggrieved by the existence of a statutory nuisance; this is likely to be a more affordable and expedient option for a person who would otherwise have to rely upon bringing an action in private nuisance or even negligence, such as in the *Hunter* case (see Section 1.3.2.2). Furthermore, construction work that is reasonably conducted does not generally constitute a private nuisance (*Andreae v. Selfridge and Co. Ltd*) although it may be a statutory nuisance. Where the complainant can convince the magistrates that there is an existing or recurring nuisance, they have a duty to serve an abatement notice requiring the defendant to abate the nuisance within a specified time, or to carry out such works so as to prevent the recurrence of the nuisance.

7.3.4. Defences for non-compliance

There are various defences which can be deployed for non-compliance with an abatement notice, but where there is no applicable defence, the person on whom the notice is served will be criminally liable for non-compliance with the notice. Section 80(7) of the EPA 1990 offers a defence where the best practical means have been used to avert the nuisance, and there is a special defence in relation to noise and nuisances on construction sites pursuant to s.80(9). This applies where the alleged nuisance is covered by a notice served under s.60 of the Control of Pollution Act 1974 (COPA 1974) or a consent given under s.61 of that Act. Conversely, if a s.60 notice has been served and its terms breached, this is indicative that a statutory nuisance has been committed pursuant to s.79 of the EPA 1990.

7.3.5. Noise under the Control of Pollution Act 1974

While COPA 1974 has been replaced for the most part by more recent legislation, the sections relating to construction noise are still in force, and s.60 applies to a wide range of construction activities from the construction and demolition of buildings to dredging work. Pursuant to this section a local authority can serve a notice which imposes certain requirements on the way in which the works are to be carried out so as to minimise noise from the construction site. The notice may specify

- hours of working
- types of plant and machinery which may or may not be used on site, and
- levels of noise which may be emitted from the site – or parts of the site – during specified hours.

It is an offence to fail to comply with a s.60 notice, and on conviction a contractor can be fined up to £2000, in addition to a daily fine of £50 for as long as the offence continues.

Under s.222 of the Local Government Act 1972, a local authority has the power to apply for an injunction against any breach of the law where it is considered 'expedient for the promotion or protection of the interests of the inhabitants of their area'. This power can be used to prevent a continuing breach of a s.60 notice, if appropriate. This power is similar to that which exists under s.81(5) of the EPA 1990 mentioned above. Although injunctions are a discretionary remedy and are not granted lightly, where the alleged nuisance is of sufficient gravity or duration, an injunction may be considered to be the only appropriate remedy. Contractors should obviously seek to avoid the risk of injunctions if at all possible on account of their potentially devastating impact on the programmed works.

Under s.61 of the COPA 1974 a contractor can apply for a consent in advance of commencing work which in effect provides a defence to a s.60 notice and the statutory nuisance provisions of the EPA 1990 (see s.80(9) of the EPA 1990). The notice represents a compromise agreed between the contractor and the local authority as to the way in which the works will be carried out so as to minimise noise. Where the terms of the s.61 consent are complied with, the local authority has no grounds for serving an abatement notice. In reality, many contractors consider application for a s.61 consent to be more trouble than it is worth because the seeking of such a consent may serve to draw attention to the site and its potential for noise, thereby encouraging the local authority to police the conditions which it has imposed. Therefore many contractors prefer to work without a consent and take the risk that the local authority will serve a s.60 notice. However, a s.61 consent may impose less onerous conditions than could accompany a s.60 notice, and the existence of and compliance with a s.61 consent can provide useful mitigating evidence against a nuisance or negligence claim from an aggrieved neighbour.

8

Insurance and lender liability

8.1. INTRODUCTION

There are three kinds of contractors' risks which are traditionally covered by insurance

- damage occurring to the works during construction
- third-party claims for personal injury or damage to property which result from carrying out of the works, and
- defects in the works, but usually only if they result from negligent design or perhaps certain other professional duties.

These risks are typically covered by a range of different types of insurance policies.

- All Risks insurance (procured either by the employer and known as 'Employers' All Risks' or 'EAR', or by the contractor and known as 'Contractors' All Risks' or 'CAR') offers cover to all the parties to a construction project primarily against damage to the works. It usually covers materials and goods on site, temporary works, plant, equipment and temporary buildings.
- Public Liability (PL) insurance is available to cover the contractor for third-party claims in respect of loss or damage to property, personal injuries and, sometimes, nuisance and interference with

easements. Such policies usually specifically exclude claims in respect of damage to the works or other matters which are intended to be addressed by All Risks policies.

- Employers' Liability (EL) insurance is available to cover the contractor against claims for injuries sustained by his employees in the course of their employment, and is in fact compulsory for all employers in the UK, at least up to the minimum limit of £5million in aggregate (under the Employers' Liability (Compulsory Insurance) Regulations 1998).
- Professional Indemnity (PI) insurance is generally taken out by construction professionals such as architects, engineers, environmental consultants and surveyors to cover their liability to pay damages to third parties – usually the client – for injury, loss or damage resulting from the insured's negligence or breach of professional duties. The requirement for construction professionals to carry adequate levels of PI insurance is a contract condition on which clients almost invariably insist. Furthermore, it is not unusual for professionals to be required to maintain cover for a specified period of time after completion of the works, which can prove costly for the professional concerned. The professional duties which are covered by such policies are generally design- or advice-related, though there are some policies which include the provision of management services. Insofar as they perform such services, contractors are also increasingly choosing, or being asked, to obtain such cover.
- Directors' and Officers' Liability (D and O) insurance is a form of personal insurance intended to indemnify those in positions of responsibility within a company against the financial effects of legal claims made against the policy-holder.

8.2. ENVIRONMENTAL RISKS AND TRADITIONAL INSURANCE POLICIES

One factor which traditional insurance policies tend to have in common is that cover for environmental pollution is generally excluded completely or extremely restricted. The insurance market is understandably wary of covering environmental risks for a number of reasons. First, environmental pollution tends to be gradual, taking place over a number of years, which means that problems often take many years to manifest themselves, making the risks particularly difficult to quantify. The original cause of pollution may be long-forgotten and the perpetrator no longer in business, which makes the recovery of any insured costs from third parties more difficult. Furthermore, the insurance industry has already paid out on some enormous environment-related claims, and its experience of asbestosis claims in America for example, has warned of the huge costs involved in covering risks for which the gestation period may span decades and where the resulting claims may arise from hundreds or even thousands of different people.

A contractor's exposure to environmental risks will vary according to the nature of the construction contract under which he is working; those engaged on traditional fixed-price or lump-sum contracts are likely to be most vulnerable in respect of claims arising out of environmental non-compliance, such as restoration costs following pollution of a watercourse and subsequent fish deaths. However, the newer types of contract such as those associated with PFI projects may expose a contractor to additional environmental liabilities. PFI contracts are commonly characterised by long concession periods and the operations covered may be environmentally-sensitive. A contractor's involvement in a PFI project may continue long after the construction works have been completed, and may involve maintenance, commissioning works and operation of the facility. The contractor is commonly expected to assume the liability for the associated environmental risks during these stages.

Further, the contractor may also be expected to accept liability for pre-existing contamination. In situations where the project is to be on a greenfield site, this risk may be reduced by the use of warranties and indemnities from the seller or landlord. However, this is less likely to be an option where the project is to be on a brownfield site, on which the public sector may have been carrying out potentially polluting activities for many years. As a generalisation, this is because one of the primary objectives of the public sector is to transfer all potential long-term liabilities. The degree of pre-existing pollution on a brownfield site is often unknown and cannot be determined, especially where there is a building on the site. Therefore, the associated environmental risks contain a large degree of uncertainty. Due to this element of uncertainty and the potentially significant costs associated with environmental risk, it is a topic on which lenders focus and accordingly apply pressure on the borrower to dilute potential liabilities. Environmental risk assignment can therefore be a 'deal breaker' in PFI negotiations.

PFI negotiations commonly start with the private sector bidder being liable for all environmental risks, as it is assumed that he has carried out his own investigations and submitted a bid accordingly. This is in line with the Treasury Taskforce Guidance on the Standardisation of PFI Contracts. However, the final contractual apportionment of liability varies in accordance with the usual commercial negotiating factors, and there are examples of the private sector shouldering 100 per cent of the environmental risk, and also vice versa, where the public sector assumes the total risk, together with multifarious apportionment arrangements between the two.

Whatever the form of contract or risk-sharing arrangement, those involved in developing sites which are potentially contaminated, or which are particularly sensitive due to the proximity of a watercourse or protected habitat, are likely to consider at least some insurance cover in respect of their environmental risks. It is not always easy to assess whether existing insurance policies provide the necessary cover, or whether a tailor-made environmental policy, which may be expensive, is required. It is important to remember that an insurance policy is simply a form of contract and it is therefore very important to read the policy wording carefully to ascertain the specific level of cover which any given policy provides. Although some policies and policy wording which are particularly widely-used have had their effect defined by the courts over the years, insurance policies are often poorly-drafted and provisions will not always mean what one might assume them to mean.

One general restriction which requires stating at the outset is that insurance cover is not available in respect of fines imposed for criminal conduct. This includes, for example, the fines imposed on companies or directors for breach of environmental statutes, such as causing polluting matter to enter controlled waters contrary to s.85 of the WRA 1991 (see Section 6.2) or disposing of waste without a licence contrary to s.33 of the EPA 1990 (see Section 5.2.3).

The more extensive All Risks policies tend to cover damage to designated property, howsoever caused, provided the risk is not specifically excluded. This means that such policies might extend to cover clean-up of pollution incidents caused by the contractor, or contaminated land remediation, if such risks were not specifically excluded. A second group of policies designed to insure the works will, however, usually identify a number of specified risks such as fire, earthquakes, flood, storms and civil commotion, against which the works will be protected. Generally the latter type of policies will not cover pollution problems unless they are precisely specified, which is highly unlikely.

Public Liability policies are general insurance policies taken out by most commercial undertakings to provide an indemnity against claims for loss or damage to third party property, personal injuries and occasionally nuisance and interference with easements. Before 1990, pollution exclusions were extremely rare because insurers appeared to consider that environmental risks were no greater than any other commercial risk, but now it is probably impossible to purchase a PL policy which does not contain some form of pollution exclusion. Typical exclusion clauses are worded as follows:

> 'This policy excludes all liability in respect of Pollution or Contamination other than caused by a sudden identifiable unintended and unexpected incident which takes place in its entirety at a specific time and place during the period of insurance.'

This means that there will be no cover for pollution resulting from gradual seepage from an underground storage tank, for example, but a sudden explosion caused by methane gas probably would be covered. One reason for excluding cover for gradual pollution is that it is often difficult to know when the polluting 'incident' occurred, which is important in occurrence-based policies such as those for PL cover (see below). However, the requirement that the incident be 'unexpected' means that the question of foreseeability comes into play, and where a contractor is building on a former landfill site, for example, it might be argued that a methane gas explosion which causes injury to third parties, or damage to third-party property is not 'unexpected'.

Professional Indemnity insurance covers professionals for claims made against them for negligence or breach of contract arising out of their work. Although this means that where pollution results from a consulting engineer's negligence, for example, clean-up costs should be covered by his PI cover, pollution exclusions are also widely used in this type of policy, and gradual pollution in particular is regularly excluded. An example of a typical exclusion clause currently used in PI and D and O policies is:

> 'Pollution whether directly or indirectly caused (including loss of value).
>
> This exclusion shall not apply where such claim or loss arises from the Insured's negligent structural design or specification or failure to report a structural defect in a property but cover shall only extend to that part of any claim or loss which relates to the cost of re-designing, re-specifying, remedying and/or rectifying the defective structure but shall not include the cost of remedying and/or rectifying any loss or damage to the land.'

One of the important differences between PI policies and PL policies is that the former tend to apply to claims made against the insured during the period of cover, while the latter cover incidents occurring during the period of cover. This is the distinction between policies written on a 'claims-made' basis and those which are on an 'occurrence' basis.

With occurrence-based policies, claims are made against the policy which is in force when the occurrence takes place, which is not necessarily the policy which is in operation at the time of the claim, though with damage resulting from sudden, one-off, incidents, the usual notification requirements will often mean that the claim *is* made during the period of cover of the policy in question. With these sorts of policies, the main issue which arises, as seen above in relation to PL policies, is whether, on their face, they are stated to exclude all or some environmental risks. The position is more complicated for claims-made policies.

With policies which operate on a claims-made basis, such as PI policies, if a claim has not been made within the year of the cover, then that policy will lapse, and, if the policy is renewed or a new policy procured, that new policy will take on the risk that a claim is made during its period of operation. The claims-made approach tends to give insurers more control over the risks which they are currently covering because of the greater disclosure which the insured can be expected to give regarding past events which are likely to give rise to claims in the future. Not only does this mean that insurers have a clearer view of the risks which they are taking on, but they also have an opportunity to exclude them from cover, or limit their exposure in respect of particular risks. Clients have generally responded to the use of claims-made policies by insisting that professionals maintain a certain level of cover for a specified number of years after the works have been completed. (It will be seen that this would not be necessary with an occurrence-based policy because the cover would endure well beyond the year in which the incident occurred.) Renewal in these circumstances can be very expensive because of the disclosure obligations which apply which mean that the insurer has greater knowledge of the risks involved, and it is important for construction professionals to be sure that they will be able to procure policies in future years before agreeing to contract conditions which oblige them to do so. The common solution is to limit the obligation to procure cover in the future to an obligation to procure cover which is available at a reasonable commercial price and on reasonable commercial conditions.

In the environmental context, the disclosure obligations provide insurers with the information they need in order to, for example, decline cover in respect of potential liabilities for known contamination. This may mean that where a site has only been partially remediated, it will not be possible to comply with a typical contractual obligation to carry insurance cover for, say, the next five years after completion of the services in question.

Even where a PI policy offers some form of cover for polluting events, it is important to remember that such policies are triggered by liability in negligence or for negligent breach of contract on the part of the professional concerned, not simply where a polluting incident has occurred. This is the case even where, for example, the mere occurrence of the incident gives rise to a liability because it amounts to a breach of contract. If the insured has used reasonable skill and care in carrying out his contractual obligations, the policy will usually not be triggered.

Furthermore, most policies only provide aggregate cover for polluting events, which means the cover could be exhausted by one large claim, leaving the insured with little or no cover for the remainder of the policy period. Pollution is unusual in this respect in that it is the only risk where the sum insured under the policy can only be used once in any policy year. In most other types of policy and for a whole range of insurable risks, each and every claim can be up to the limit of the policy, no matter how many claims are made in the policy year.

While a number of environmental statutes contain provisions which can impose personal criminal liability on directors and other senior personnel for the errors and omissions of their company, D and O insurance generally excludes liability arising in connection with pollution. Section 157 of the Environmental Protection Act 1990, for example, provides that where a company has committed an offence under the Act and it is proved:

> '...to have been committed with the consent or connivance of, or to have been attributable to any neglect on the part of, any director, manager, secretary or other similar officer of the body corporate or a person who was purporting to act in any such capacity...'

that person should also be guilty of the offence and liable to be punished accordingly. Unfortunately, traditional D and O insurance will not generally assist in such circumstances because 'off-the-shelf' policies invariably contain pollution exclusions, although as the market has matured there are a growing number of underwriters prepared to provide tailor-made policies to provide pollution cover for directors and others in positions of responsibility for environmental matters. There are now several underwriters who can offer cover in respect of a director's personal assets and any legal costs and expenses incurred in defending criminal proceedings. However, as mentioned above, cover is not available in respect of any criminal fine which may be imposed as a penalty for commission of an environmental offence, and clearly it cannot assist in the event that a prison sentence is demanded.

8.3. ENVIRONMENTAL IMPAIRMENT LIABILITY INSURANCE

It is apparent from the above analysis, that there are limits to the level of comfort which can be derived by a contractor from one of his traditional insurance policies in respect of cover for environmental risks, unless he is very confident that the type of risks to which he might be exposed are not excluded. The implementation of the new contaminated land regime (Part IIA of the EPA 1990, see further Chapter 4) has meant that a contractor now faces a greater risk of being held liable for the clean-up costs of contaminated land, either as a polluter or occupier. This is particularly pertinent in the case of PFI projects, where the contractor's involvement is likely to be more long term.

To obtain cover for pollution claims it is generally necessary to obtain specialised Environmental Impairment Liability (EIL) insurance. These policies have been written specifically to provide cover in an area of the insurance market where there has traditionally been very little. Most EIL policies cover the following

- gradual pollution, both on-site and off-site, where pollution has migrated
- pollution which has originated off-site and migrated on-site
- full civil liability, including bodily injury and economic loss
- legal costs for criminal liability, and
- personal liability for the directors and officers of a company.

There is a range of different policies available to suit the requirements of the various parties who may be involved; contractors, landowners, consultants, lenders etc. Options include annual policies, which are more suited to low-risk projects, and long-term policies of up to 25 years. Some insurers offer a policy option for a particular project, which consists of a fixed-price premium that is freely transferable between specified parties for a defined period. This means insurance can be transferred on sale of all or part of the land. This is particularly useful as contracts of sale for industrial or other potentially-contaminated sites will often include a requirement on the purchaser to maintain certain levels of insurance cover in respect of environmental risks. In addition, there are policies that allow for changes in the law. Most EIL policies acknowledge that an environmental 'incident' may result in injury or impairment to a number of sites and/or a number of people. However, the insurance industry has sought to limit its exposure through the introduction of a limit per claim under such policies, and/or a total aggregate limit for the policy year.

In their infancy, EIL policies were seen as very expensive in relation to the amount of cover which they offered the insured. However, competition within the insurance industry and increasing amounts of environmental information available to the insurer has meant that the premiums have reduced, the amount of cover has increased and policies have become more flexible. The availability of EIL policies has also had a positive impact on deals which were so entrenched in potential environmental liability, that a successful commercial outcome might otherwise have been unachievable. As a consequence of these positive factors, it would seem that the take-up of specialist or bespoke policies is increasing, and as more companies realise that traditional PL and PI policies in particular do not provide the type of cover which clients are increasingly demanding, it seems likely that use of EIL insurance will become more widespread.

EIL insurance is invariably site-specific and dependent upon a detailed environmental assessment of the site and the operations to be carried out there, in order that the insurer can make an adequate assessment of the risk. This assessment not only focuses on the current and proposed operations, but also considers historic usage of the site. An assessment is usually carried out by the insurer's risk assessor, using a combination of modern technology and the insured's or seller's existing environmental reports. This will often avoid the necessity for a full site investigation, which can be costly. Where there is no existing environmental information, the insurer may be content to rely on a 'Phase One' or desk-top survey of the site. However, in addition to this there are of course onerous requirements on the insured regarding disclosure. In reality this tends to mean that companies which can qualify for EIL insurance – because they have clean, well-run sites with no obvious environmental problems – probably have considerably less need for it than those that cannot!

Contractors seeking EIL cover are likely to have the additional problem that they will require permission from the client to have the necessary site assessment carried out, and he may not be keen to have any problems relating to the condition of the site highlighted, for fear that he could be held criminally liable subsequently for 'knowingly permitting' pollution to occur. However, where existing environmental information is available about a site, insurers are increasingly prepared to rely on this alone, provided that the source of information is considered reliable.

EIL policies tend to be written on a 'claims-made' basis, which avoids the problems of defining when a pollution incident has occurred. However, because the policies are written on a 'claims-made' basis the insured immediately loses the benefit of the cover as soon as the policy expires, even for events which occurred during the period of the policy, if no claim was made during that period. Some policies go further and require that the event must be reported to the insurer and the claim made during the period. In order to mitigate the consequences of this, most EIL policies can be extended — usually on payment of an additional premium — so as to respond to claims based upon events which have occurred during the period of the policy and which are notified to the insurer within a set period, such as six months or a year beyond the expiry of that policy.

8.4. INVESTMENT AND LENDER LIABILITY

The attitude of lenders to projects which may have a significant environmental impact, or which involve remediation of contamination prior to construction, tends to be extremely conservative.

Lenders are largely concerned for three reasons.

• The first concern is the indirect impact which onerous environmental liability may have on them, if it prevents the borrower from meeting his repayment obligations.

- A second, and more direct, concern stems from the fact that if a site turns out to be heavily contaminated this may mean that its value is inadequate security for the loan, meaning that the lender is vulnerable if the borrower defaults.
- The third concern is currently more anticipated than actual, but relates to the fact that in the USA banks and lending institutions have been targetted as 'deep pockets' when clean-up is required and those directly responsible for the pollution cannot afford the remediation costs.

Under existing UK legislation lenders are only likely to be primarily liable for pollution offences where they can be deemed to have caused or knowingly permitted the pollution. Although it is possible to envisage circumstances where lenders are sufficiently closely involved with the everyday activities of a company which causes pollution, so as to be deemed to have knowingly permitted the pollution, this is fairly unlikely to occur where a bank has simply loaned money to the owner or developer of contaminated land.

However, as discussed in Section 4.2, the contaminated land regime implemented by Part IIa of the EPA 1990, has the potential to impose liability for the cost of land remediation on the owner or occupier of the site for the time being, where the original polluter cannot be found. The definition of 'owner' specifically includes mortgagees in possession, although it is unclear at present whether those who lend money using other funding mechanisms will be caught in a similar manner. Similarly the statutory nuisance provisions set out in Part III of the EPA 1990, which are discussed in detail in Chapter 7, impose liability on the owner or occupier of the land if the instigator of the nuisance cannot be found.

Under English law there are four ways in which a lender might enforce a mortgage

- sale
- receivership
- taking possession, and
- foreclosure.

A sale will not render a mortgagee an occupier, but taking possession of mortgaged land, or taking possession of a debt by serving notice on the debtor to pay him rather than the mortgagor, might. Where a mortgagee takes possession of a rental stream for example, he effectively becomes an owner. Similarly foreclosure – which requires a Court Order – will make the mortgagee the owner of the mortgaged land, although where a receiver is appointed, the receiver will not be classed as an owner because in legal terms he is usually defined as acting as the agent of the mortgagor. A receiver might constitute an occupier but the new contaminated land regime (see Section 4.2) includes a specific exemption for receivers whereby they will not be liable for clean-up costs for contaminated land unless they have acted in a way that is deemed unreasonable in their capacity as a receiver.

Lenders face something of a dilemma in the context of environmental liability. If they behave 'responsibly' and commission an environmental audit of a business and then insist that the auditor's recommendations are carried out as part of the conditions on which a loan is granted to the business, it might be argued that the lending institution is exercising a degree of control over the company and perhaps is acting as a shadow director. On the other hand, if a bank does not make any enquiries about the environmental performance of a company – and therefore cannot be accused of having any degree of control in that area of the company's business – the bank may risk incurring a bad debt through ignorance of the true state of a company's environmental liabilities. The definition of a shadow director is generally taken to mean any person in accordance with whose directions or instructions the directors of a company are accustomed to act (see for example, s.741(2) of the Companies Act 1985, and s.251 of the Insolvency Act 1986).

In the context of PFI projects where a Special Purpose Company (SPC) is the usual vehicle through which funding is channelled, lenders will seek to ensure that any risks taken on by the SPC – such as an indemnity given to a public authority in respect of remediation of contaminated land – are passed on in their entirety to contractors or sub-contractors working for the SPC. Where some residual liability remains with the SPC, lenders might require the SPC to procure insurance to cover any potential future claims in order to secure the loan and their return on it.

In more traditional projects lenders do not usually have the added protection of an SPC by way of a liability 'backstop'. Nonetheless, lenders involved in projects where there is considered to be an increased level of environmental risk will generally insist on a range of precautionary measures, including completion of a thorough site investigation and adequate provision for contingencies such as discovering the presence of a leaking underground storage tank or some other hazard. Other uncertainties for lenders – as well as for contractors – include the problem of costing reclamation schemes; where more extensive contamination is discovered than initially expected, the project can be delayed and go over budget.

Furthermore, there is always the fear that clean-up standards will vary over time, or that legislation will change – to include retrospective liability for example – and that this will lead to unforeseen liabilities. Such concerns have been largely fuelled by the experience of lenders in the USA where there have been a number of cases of perceived 'deep pockets' being found liable for environmental clean-up costs, under a legal regime which imposes retrospective and joint and several liability for environmental pollution. However, legislative changes of this type in the UK seem unlikely not only because they would be politically unpopular, but also because there is little indication that the US system is actually leading to an effective clean-up of that country's contaminated land. The result of joint and several liability is that the potentially responsible parties (PRPs) spend years involved in costly litigation trying to demonstrate that they were not responsible – or were perhaps only 10% responsible – for the liability in question.

Before advancing any funds, a lending institution will usually want to assure itself of the following

- the past environmental performance of the borrower
- the management attitudes of the borrower to protection of the environment, and
- what, if any, environmental warranties the borrower has given or received.

Potential lenders will also be alive to the fact that environmental liabilities may not be limited to the activities of the present owner or borrower, and where appropriate, borrowers will be encouraged to seek indemnities in respect of environmental problems which result from the activities of previous owners of the land in question. Similarly a borrower is generally not advised to give indemnities to subsequent purchasers of the land against clean-up costs which result from activities of a previous owner.

While there are a number of banks and lending institutions who are prepared to lend on projects which carry significant environmental risks, getting a loan on such schemes may be a more lengthy process than with more straightforward projects, and may involve greater initial outlay of capital.

9

Crisis management

9.1. INTRODUCTION

Every organisation fervently hopes that it will never have to deal with a crisis of any type. However, common sense dictates that things can go seriously wrong very quickly at any time for anyone, often in ways that could not have been anticipated. Companies cannot be expected to be prepared for every eventuality, but there are a number of steps which can be taken to plan for foreseeable problems. In addition, having a set of procedures in place which can be applied in almost any circumstances will enable some level of order to be imposed in the event of an unanticipated crisis. Forewarned is forearmed. This Chapter will look at

- what constitutes a crisis in the environmental context
- managing an environmental crisis in a correct and efficient way
- powers of the regulatory authorities
- interviews under caution
- legal obligations and requirements following a polluting incident
- managing protester action, and
- establishing a set of procedures to be followed in the immediate aftermath of a crisis.

9.2. WHAT IS A CRISIS?

A crisis is an occurrence or event that can have detrimental consequences for a business. In the context of the environment, the impact of a crisis may be instantly apparent, or the full effects of a crisis might only become evident after a period of time.

Examples of crises which are immediately apparent include

- an environmental incident such as the spillage of a large volume of pollutants (e.g. chemicals or diesel) into the soil or a nearby water source which, in turn, may contaminate a local drinking water source
- a serious health and safety incident on-site involving employees and/or members of the public such as collapsing scaffolding, or
- environmental protesters staging demonstrations on or near the site of business.

Examples of crises which can develop over time include

- incorrect storage of hazardous substances or other contaminants which permits leakage of the substances over time causing contamination of the soil and/or groundwater, or
- legal proceedings relating to exposure to hazardous substances brought by current and/or former employees, for example, asbestosis claims.

A crisis may arise directly as a result of action or inaction on the part of the business or indirectly as a result of the action or inaction of a third party over which the affected business has little or no control.

9.3. MANAGING AN ENVIRONMENTAL CRISIS

There is no general legal requirement obliging companies to establish criteria to be followed in the event of a crisis, although certain industries which are deemed to be 'high risk' for reasons of significant quantities of hazardous substances produced, stored or handled on site are required to prepare emergency plans, pursuant to the Control of Major Accident Hazards Regulations 1999 (COMAH Regulations).

The Nuclear Installations Act 1965 imposes a similar obligation on the nuclear industry. The Management of Health and Safety at Work Regulations 1999 require employers to establish and where necessary give effect to appropriate procedures to be followed in the event of an emergency involving serious and imminent danger to persons at work, but this requirement would not cover risks to the environment which did not endanger personnel.

In practice, however, it is prudent to draw up a suitable internal policy with a view to minimising legal liability and adverse publicity in the event of a crisis. This plan should work in conjuction with, or form part of, the business emergency and disaster recovery plans. It is important to ensure that the relevant persons at the appropriate levels in the business are appraised of its contents. The relevant individuals will generally be site management given that they are charged with the responsibility of overseeing and co-ordinating work on-site. Site managers are usually in the best position to know what is happening on-site and whether the site is in compliance with legal requirements including, for example, conditions of environmental consents.

As soon as work has started on-site the possibility of an environmental crisis occurring exists. It is therefore vital that site management is aware of

- the necessary steps to be taken to minimise or mitigate the potential adverse effects of an incident
- the legal implications, if any, of an incident, and
- the legal obligations, if any, in relation to an incident.

Provision of this type of information to the relevant individuals can be usefully done as part of an Environmental Management System. Whatever the chosen approach, establishing specific procedures to be implemented on the occurrence of a crisis is beneficial to the business as a whole and serves to ensure that on-site works and the operation of a business continue to run as smoothly as possible. Below are some examples of the advantages of having set procedures and guidelines in place.

- A business could avoid potential delays in completion of a project which, in turn, could save costs.
- A business could avoid potential prosecution, fines, payment of damages, and even revocation of licences/consents.
- A business could establish a co-operative relationship with environmental regulators in respect of existing and future projects.
- It enhances the public's view of the organisation.
- It is attractive to current and potential clients who appreciate the ever-increasing importance of the role of the environment in business and who are conscious of the value of good practice management.
- It creates a comfortable and safe environment for employees.

While procedures and guidelines will be tailored to the individual business in terms of its operations and management structure, there are certain generalisations which can be made.

- Who will 'manage' the crisis — employees should be familiar with the chain of command.
- Determine who should be informed and in what order; senior managers and relatives of possible victims should not learn of the crisis via the media.
- Information being given to third parties should be channelled through one spokesperson to ensure consistency — determine who this should be, and in their absence, an alternative.
- Where remediation measures need to be implemented quickly make sure that contact details for relevant contractors or equipment specialists are available.
- Try to envisage a 'worst-case scenario' and make contingencies.
- Regular training and exercises (e.g. table-top scenarios) ensure that everyone knows how the policy works in practice.

Where an incident could lead to prosecution (either of the company or individuals) there are a number of a steps which if taken at the outset, could persuade an enforcing authority not to prosecute

- prepare an internal investigation report: the style and content is a matter which needs to be determined having regard to (i)

management requirements, (ii) the interests of insurers, (iii) the usual undesirability of admissions of liability pending certainty as to the position, and (iv) issues connected with the rules governing legal professional privilege; as to all of these matters, lawyers should be consulted

- consider the need for independent expert evidence, and obtain prompt specialist legal advice
- take a view on the likely outcome of the incident to determine the appropriate approach to the regulator (see Section 9.6 below)
- uncover the 'paper trail' to identify any relevant documentation
- where remediation measures are possible seek to implement them immediately, and
- record all actions taken (and costs) for future reference.

Such points should feature in the management guidelines laid down for handling a crisis of this type. Company procedures need to be drafted in the light of regulatory authorities' powers (detailed below); in this way employees can be briefed on how to respond to requests for information or direct questions posed by the regulatory inspector.

9.4. REGULATORY POWERS OF ENFORCING AUTHORITIES

Generally there are no reporting requirements under environmental legislation in England and Wales, i.e. in circumstances where a polluting incident occurs, the polluter is not obliged to report the incident to the regulatory authorities. However, there are exceptions to this rule

- the COMAH Regulations state that the 'competent authority' (which is the Health and Safety Executive and the Environment Agency acting jointly) must be informed in the event that a major accident occurs (Regulation 15(3) and (4)), and
- the Nuclear Installations Act 1965 imposes a similar reporting obligation on nuclear installation operators.

While only operators of potentially hazardous installations are covered by a reporting requirement under environmental legislation, the requirement to report breaches of health and safety legislation is more commonplace.

So far as the investigation of any incidents is concerned (whether reported or not), in the context of environmental regulation the Environment Agency is usually the relevant enforcing authority. The powers of the Agency and other enforcing authorities have been essentially consolidated in the Environment Act 1995 (the 1995 Act), and include powers of entry (s.108), power to deal with the cause of imminent danger of serious pollution (s.109), offences (s.110), gathering of evidence (s.111) and disclosure of information (s.113). These powers are exercised through the medium of an Authorised Person.

Regulatory authorities have the power under the 1995 Act to authorise suitable persons (Authorised Person), on the satisfaction of certain conditions, to enter premises with a view to assessing whether the premises in question are in compliance with environmental legislation. This authorisation to enter premises must be in writing, but the decision as to which premises it is necessary to enter rests with the Authorised Person who will usually be an Environment Agency officer, but in theory can be anyone that the Secretary of State or the Environment Agency deems to be 'suitable' (s.108).

Given the range of offences covered in the 1995 Act it is advisable to confirm with the authorities which powers they are invoking to investigate and bear in mind the Dos and Don'ts Checklist at Section 9.8.

An Authorised Person may exercise the following powers in accordance with the terms of a written authorisation

- enter premises at reasonable times (save in emergency, when immediate entry is permissible) which the Authorised Person has reason to believe it is necessary for him to enter (s.108(4)(a))
- take another Authorised Person (and if serious obstruction is anticipated, a police officer) and also any requisite equipment or materials required for the purposes of carrying out an investigation (s.108(4)(b))
- carry out examinations and investigations as are necessary in the circumstances (s.108(4)(c))

- direct that the premises or its contents be left undisturbed as long as necessary for the purpose of the investigation (s.108(4)(d))
- take measurements and photographs and make recordings (s.108(4)(e))
- take samples of air, water or land on or in the vicinity of the premises (s.108(4)(f))
- dismantle or test articles or substances found on the premises which appear to have caused or are likely to cause pollution to the environment or human health (s.108(4)(g))
- take possession of and detain articles or substances for the purposes of examination or use as evidence in a prosecution (s.108(4)(h))
- require a person to answer questions and sign a declaration as to the truth of his answers (s.108(4)(j))
- require the production of records or extracts therefrom and inspect and take copies of such reports insofar as they are within the control of the person (s.108(4)(k))
- require that a person provide facilities and assistance, (s.108(4)(l)), and
- such other matters as may be prescribed by regulations under the 1995 Act (s.108(4)(m)).

These extensive powers are counterbalanced by numerous safeguards against abuse by the regulatory authorities. Except in the case of an emergency, at least seven days notice must be given to the person who appears to be the occupier of the premises. The consent of the occupier is required prior to entry, unless the situation is deemed by the Authorised Person to be an emergency. Where the consent of the occupier is not forthcoming a warrant may be obtained by the enforcing authorities. These powers of entry cannot be used to compel the production of a document which a person is entitled to withhold on the grounds of legal professional privilege. Answers given to questions posed by the Authorised Person (other than under caution) cannot be used as evidence in criminal proceedings against that person or their spouse, although information gleaned this way can be used against third-parties, including employers.

The 1995 Act permits Authorised Persons carrying out investigations to seize and render harmless any article or substance which appears to be capable of causing imminent pollution or serious harm to human health. In the event that this power is used by an Authorised Person, a report must be drafted and signed by the Authorised Person and copies provided to the relevant person at the premises and the owner of the premises.

It is important to note that it is an offence to obstruct intentionally a person carrying out their duties under the 1995 Act where the Authorised Person is charged with investigating an incident which could cause imminent danger of serious pollution or harm to human health. It is also an offence to fail to comply, without a reasonable excuse, with any of the requirements under the 1995 Act, such as the provision of facilities, assistance or information as and when requested by the Authorised Person. Given the criminal nature of failing to co-operate with an investigation, it is usually prudent to assist the regulatory authorities insofar as is possible with all aspects of any investigation. However, this is an aspect which needs to be approached with care and having regard to the particular circumstances of each case. For those who are inexperienced in reacting to such situations, the assistance of a lawyer is indispensable in making the relevant judgements.

9.5. INTERVIEWS UNDER CAUTION

Prosecution of employees is very rare but possible in some circumstances (see, for example, the discussion in Section 1.3.1 on personal liability). However, corporate defendants need to decide who will speak on behalf of the company. Depending on the personnel in question it may be necessary to send along two people to be interviewed – one to speak 'officially' on behalf of the company and someone with more 'hands-on' knowledge who will be in a position to brief the other on matters that arise in questions. It is essential to prepare for interviews most thoroughly; hours if not days should be spent gathering the relevant information on procedures, events and contracts and so on.

Where an employee is required by the enforcing authority to provide a statement under statutory powers (such as s.115(8) of the EPA 1990) he has the right to be cautioned, in other words, informed that he is facing criminal prosecution and that his statement may be used in evidence. If he is not cautioned he is entitled to rely on the privilege against self-incrimination. However, this principle does not prevent the enforcing authority from obtaining and using statements provided by a company's employees as evidence against others, such as the company or its directors. The Environment Agency uses interviews under caution as a means of gathering evidence for a possible prosecution, whether of an individual or of the company. In practice, it may not appear to an employee that the 'chat' he has had with the enforcing authority constituted an interview under caution. For this reason, companies are advised to ensure that site personnel who might be questioned by the Environment Agency in the event of a pollution incident, for example, have a proper understanding of what is likely to occur and how to react, and are properly supported and advised. It is prudent to instruct a solicitor to be present during any interview to be conducted under caution. Points which can arise and which should be discussed with the company's lawyer include

- when employees are being interviewed under caution, they should understand the significance of the statement which they give
- it is essential to ascertain the capacity in which the individual is being interviewed; i.e. is it the intention to prosecute the individual or the company? Similarly, it is necessary for the interviewer to appreciate the capacity of the interviewee. This should be confirmed both before the interview is arranged and again for the purposes of the interview record
- if a company instructs a solicitor to act, is it on behalf of the company or the individual? Both may be needed
- where an individual seems potentially exposed to personal criminal charges — rare as that may be — he should usually be advised to obtain separate legal advice. Sometimes the company will decide to

pay the legal costs by way of assistance to the individual and, in appropriate cases, there is nothing wrong in principle with doing so

- the company needs to decide who has authority to speak on its behalf — usually a director or senior manager with particular responsibility for the area of work in question
- the company should ascertain what charges are being considered by the enforcing authority in order to prepare and provide any defences it may have
- the company or its solicitor is advised to approach the enforcing authority prior to the interview in order to gather information about what questions are likely to be asked. The enforcing authority is not obliged to provide this information (*R v. Imran and Hussain*) but it is usually worth ascertaining as much as possible with the aim of avoiding surprises, e.g. know which employees were questioned immediately after the event, and what evidence the authority may have gleaned from them
- if the company intends to plead guilty, it is often useful to get this on record, make an apology and introduce mitigation. Make sure that the interviewee can respond to all aggravating factors, such as suggestions of cost-cutting
- if the company intends to plead not guilty, or is still undecided, it is preferable to make sure the interviewee does not admit liability, but introduces defence and mitigation evidence, and again responds to all aggravating factors
- where a potential interviewee is thought unlikely to be able to cope with the pressure of an interview under caution the authority may accept a written statement by way of response, rendering an interview unnecessary.

There is no right to be interviewed. Lack of an interview can be a problem when defending liability and also when mitigating. In certain circumstances it may actually be appropriate to ask for an interview in an effort to persuade the regulatory authority that a prosecution is not necessary. Bearing in mind the Environment Agency's *Enforcement and Prosecution Policy* and the Functional Guidelines (see further Section 1.4.1) any attempt to pursuade the Agency that prosecution may not be required should focus on factors which may assist the company's case, such as the lack of resultant harm, the company's previously good record and so on.

9.6. POLLUTING INCIDENTS

A polluting incident in the context of crisis management will usually involve the contamination of soil, water (including groundwater) or air by hazardous substances (for example, asbestos, diesel, chemicals) used in the operation of a business or which are stored on-site prior to use in the operation of a business.

9.6.1. Action to take on occurrence of polluting incident

The fact that there are no reporting requirements does not mean that a polluter will avoid detection, liability for clean-up costs, or even criminal liability provided for under environmental legislation. The lack of a requirement to report does not prevent a polluter from reporting an incident voluntarily. The legislation provides no direct guidance as to what steps should be undertaken on the occurrence of a polluting incident, only that a polluter will be responsible for a polluting incident. Therefore, the question arises — what should a responsible company do?

The answer to this question depends on the nature and extent of the polluting incident. Where the incident is a serious one whereby there is an imminent threat of serious harm being caused to the environment or to human health, it may be wise to be proactive by reporting the incident to the regulatory authorities. The polluter will then have the opportunity to liaise and co-operate with the regulatory authorities in drawing up an action plan for the purposes of cleaning up the site to a standard required under environmental legislation (usually to the standard of being suitable for use). The reaction of the regulatory authorities to such voluntary action will vary from region to region. Proactivity is not a guarantee of avoiding the requisite penalties provided for under environmental legislation, however, it may be sufficiently persuasive to convince the regulatory authorities that a Formal Caution as opposed to a prosecution may be more appropriate in the circumstances. Any mitigating factors which can be relied upon – such as prompt admission of liability or an undertaking to remedy the situation – may assist the regulatory authority in deciding how it should exercise its broad discretion in relation to a specific offence (see further Section 1.4.1 and the Environment Agency's 'Functional Guidelines').

In the event that the incident is of a minor nature and is capable of being managed without advice from the regulatory authorities, it may be thought that there is no need to notify the incident. Such minor incidents may be capable of being addressed with the assistance of environmental consultants.

9.6.2. Recording polluting incidents

All incidents, whether minor or major, should be recorded with a view to creating a paper trail in the event that the incident is ever investigated, legal proceedings brought in respect thereof or the site sold. Other information should include details of action taken by the business. Correspondence with the Environment Agency and any legal or expert environmental advice should be retained. A report of the incident should be drafted and its contents discussed amongst site management with a view to preventing a repeat of the incident in the future. A review of the relevant procedures should be undertaken and amendments made where appropriate. A repeat incident may be sufficient to persuade the Agency to prosecute where otherwise a Formal Caution might have been deemed an adequate sanction (see Section 1.4.1).

Having said all of this, a discussion with lawyers will assist in deciding how far the company ought to arrange its affairs so that legal professional privilege attaches to documents which it brings into existence in relation to an incident. This can result in such documents becoming non-disclosable so far as regulatory or enforcement authorities are concerned. Again, these are matters which should be discussed and decided having regard to the facts of the case in question. Having said this, it is useful to develop some standard procedures concerning such matters in advance.

9.6.3. Expert advice

Initial decisions made in respect of a polluting incident will be very important in shaping whether a confrontational or a co-operative approach with the enforcing authorities will be taken and, ultimately, the approach the enforcing authorities will adopt.

It is advisable to seek legal advice on the occurrence of a polluting incident irrespective of the scale of the incident. Prompt advice can be provided as to whether the regulatory authorities should be notified or whether it will suffice to instruct environmental consultants to assess the situation. Environmental lawyers will often have a very good 'feel' for the approach generally taken by the enforcing authorities with regard to polluting incidents and often have a long-established professional relationship with the regulatory authorities. It is often best to instruct them to act as the main point of contact with the enforcing authorities.

Suitably-qualified and experienced environmental consultants may be instructed on appropriate terms and conditions with a view to assessing the full extent and potential clean-up costs of the incident. It will be the environmental consultants who will be best placed to work in conjunction with the regulatory authorities' experts with regard to the drafting of an action plan for clean-up. The lawyers and environmental consultants should liaise closely on progress and report back to the client on a regular basis.

9.7. PROTESTER ACTION AND THE ENVIRONMENT

Organised protests by environmentalists campaigning against the potential for adverse environmental consequences arising from the activities of industry, including the construction industry, are becoming a familiar and ever-frequent occurrence. Protests are often peaceful, although protesters may gain access to a site by force (trespassing), obstruct the passage of vehicles of a business and may even cause criminal damage. In such circumstances what option does the target business (Target) have?

Generally, construction contracts grant possession of the site to the contractor. Unless otherwise provided, the other party to the contract – usually the employer – must provide unhindered possession of the site. Where an employer permits a contractor to take possession of a site where protesters are already *in situ*, the employer will generally be in breach of contract.

If, on the other hand, the protesters gain access to the site after the employer has handed over possession to the contractor, the contractor may be expected to assume any subsequent risks. A contractor in lawful possession of land has the following options.

Before protesters enter site/obstruct transport
Under English law an application can be made to the High Court or County Court for a prohibitory injunction. An injunction can be obtained at short notice and is aimed at preventing protesters accessing the Target's site or obstructing transport vehicles. Where the application is successful and the injunction is obtained the protesters will be required to abide by its terms, otherwise they will be in contempt of court and liable for fines and/or imprisonment.

This type of prohibitory injunction is only granted where a threatened incursion is certain or imminent. To obtain a prohibitory injunction there must be sufficient proof of imminent damage and it must be demonstrated that if the activity were to continue the damage accruing would be significant enough to make it difficult to rectify. Bell and McGillivray (see *Ball and Bell on Environmental Law*, 5th Edition, 2000) note that such injunctions are rarely granted, in any event.

Once protesters are in situ
Under UK law trespass is not generally a criminal wrong and is not,

therefore, a matter in which the police will become involved. However, many statutes provide that specific forms of trespass or trespass on specific types of property *are* criminal or are components of more widely-defined offences.

Thus, for example, Part V of the Criminal Justice and Public Order Act 1994 provides for criminal liability in connection with collective trespass to land. Section 68 of this Part provides an offence of 'Aggravated Trespass' which may be appropriate in the context of certain environmental protest actions. Section 68(1) states:

> 'A person commits the offence of aggravated trespass if he trespasses on land in the open air and, in relation to any lawful activity which persons are engaging in or are about to engage in on that or adjoining land in the open air, does there anything which is intended by him to have the effect —
>
> > (a) of intimidating those persons or any of them so as to deter them or any of them from engaging in that activity,
> >
> > (b) of obstructing that activity, or
> >
> > (c) of disrupting that activity.'

Once protesters have accessed a site of which the Target is physically in possession, the Target may legally remove them insofar as no more force than is reasonably necessary is used (usually undertaken by a security team). If protesters enter peacefully they must first be requested to leave. Where protesters access a site with force or violence the Target is permitted to remove them without a prior request to leave. It is very important to note that the Target may be guilty of trespass to a person or other actionable wrongs if it uses more force than is considered reasonable.

There are a number of different types of applications which can be made to the courts with a view to requiring the protesters to vacate the site. Where the requirements of such injunctions are ignored by the protesters who refuse to leave, the Target may apply for a writ or a warrant for possession. This is delivered to the sheriff or bailiff who has the authority to evict the protesters from the site.

In addition, the Target has statutory powers and common-law powers of arrest. Statutory powers contained within s.24 of the Police and Criminal Evidence Act 1984 permit the Target to arrest without a warrant

- persons in the act of, or persons whom it has reasonable grounds for suspecting are committing an arrestable offence (e.g. theft and all serious offences against the person),
- persons who have, or persons whom it has reasonable grounds for suspecting have, committed an arrestable offence.

The definition of those offences which are classed as 'arrestable' for the purposes of s.24 are numerous and wide-ranging; they include theft, carrying an offensive weapon, and harassment.

In practice, the Target will usually call the police rather than rely on a security team.

Nonetheless, common law powers permit the Target to arrest a person for breach of the peace, which can mean criminal damage, assault etc.

- where such breach is committed in the presence of the arresting person (usually the security team) or
- where the arresting person honestly and reasonably believes such a breach will be committed in his presence. This is an exceptional power and should only be used in circumstances where it is apparent that such a breach is a real danger.

In practice the Target would be ill-advised to attempt to exercise these powers unless extremely confident of its position – their unlawful exercise could lead to charges of assault and false imprisonment. Furthermore, the police obviously have more scope in exercising their powers of arrest. Given police training and experience it will almost invariably be preferable to allow them to handle such situations. However, whether the Target decides to manage the protester action internally or call in the police it will be crucial for the Target to balance the effects of either approach from a public relations perspective whilst bearing in mind the nature, extent and the mood of the protesters.

Targets can prepare a plan of action in anticipation of protester action, especially where a specific business is frequently subjected to such action. The relevant persons in the Target should be appraised of how such action is to be carried out, what is permitted within the scope of the law and when it is necessary to get the police involved. It is worth noting that as a result of the Human Rights Act 1998 (HRA 1998) which came into force in 2000 protesters may be in a position to rely on more extensive rights than are currently available to them under domestic legislation regarding freedom of expression and association. It is yet to be seen how certain rights enshrined in the HRA 1998 will impact on UK legislation.

9.8. ENVIRONMENTAL CRISIS MANAGEMENT – A SUMMARY

Environmental Crisis Management
Do's and Don'ts

POWERS OF ENFORCING AUTHORITIES

DO	DON'T
Ascertain which powers are being relied on to gain entry to investigate	
Confirm Authorised Person has been authorised by the enforcing authority in writing	
Co-operate with the investigation (including providing consent to enter premises as soon as practicable)	Obstruct the investigation or any member of the regulatory authority
Provide personal details, i.e. name, address and job title	Volunteer any further information or documentation
Ensure that anyone interviewed is accompanied throughout their interview by another person from the business/site	Agree to an interview alone
Draft a detailed record of the investigation and include such details as	
• name of investigating person	
• title	
• date	
• time	
• duration of investigation	
• areas of premises which were of particular interest to the investigating person	
• details of any samples taken, i.e. from where were the samples taken?	
• weather conditions on that day, and	
• any other facts of interest.	
For these purposes a standard form could be drawn up	
Seek legal advice where unsure about scope of powers or exercise of powers of investigation	

ACTION ON OCCURRENCE OF POLLUTING INCIDENTS

DO	DON'T
Seek expert advice (legal and environmental)	Try to 'hush-up' a major incident
Notify regulatory authorities in respect of a major incident with a view to ascertaining requirements for clean-up	
Log polluting incidents in incident report book	
Retain all correspondence and information relating to incident as a 'paper trail'	
Analyse possible cause of polluting incidents. Review and update relevant procedures and crisis management guidelines where necessary	
Think of public relations consequences of action proposed	

PROTESTER ACTION

DO	DON'T
Prior to taking possession of a site ascertain whether there are any protesters/trespassers present	Take possession of a site which protesters have accessed until employer exercises rights to remove protesters
Assess the 'mood' of the protest, i.e. aggressive or peaceful	Aggravate the situation by taking an aggressive approach from the outset, especially where evident that protesters are peaceful and reasonable
Try to reason with protesters and request them to leave	
Train staff responsible for dealing with protesters (security team) how to handle protesters. Staff must be informed of what can be done legally in such circumstances	
If business is continually targeted by protesters it is possible to have the legal documents required to obtain injuctions in place in anticipation of obtaining injunctions where required	Work on environmentally-sensitive projects without calculating – and making allowance for – the commercial risk of dealing with protesters
Weigh up how best to deal with the protesters, i.e. security team or police	
Think about the public relations consequences of how protesters will be handled	

10

Proactive project planning

In addition to being a brief summary of the preceding chapers, the following checklists are intended to provide a loosely chronological *aide-mémoire* for project managers involved in proactive project planning.

Pre-contract checklist

☐ Has the proposed development got an appropriate planning consent? If not
  - pre-submission discussions with planning authority
  - completion of application form
  - supporting plans/statement, and
  - cheque for fees.

☐ Is it necessary to carry out an EIA? If so
  - pre-submission discussions/scoping opinion from planning authority
  - appointment of appropriate consultants
  - consultation with statutory/non-statutory consultees, and
  - preparation of environmental statement.

☐ Has a checklist been carried out to determine whether or not the site is contaminated (cf. risk of being a Class B appropriate person)? Desk-top site study — if possible contamination, then
  - appointment of appropriate consultants
  - risk assessment, and
  - contractual apportionment of liability.

☐ Is a Waste Management Licence needed? If yes
  - completion of application form, and
  - cheque for fees.

continued on following page

Pre-contract checklist continued

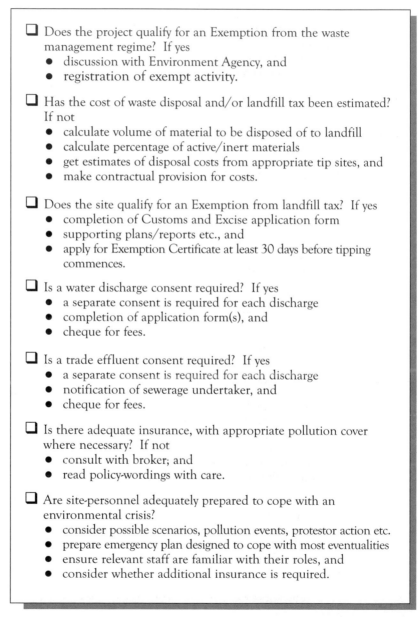

❑ Does the project qualify for an Exemption from the waste management regime? If yes
- discussion with Environment Agency, and
- registration of exempt activity.

❑ Has the cost of waste disposal and/or landfill tax been estimated? If not
- calculate volume of material to be disposed of to landfill
- calculate percentage of active/inert materials
- get estimates of disposal costs from appropriate tip sites, and
- make contractual provision for costs.

❑ Does the site qualify for an Exemption from landfill tax? If yes
- completion of Customs and Excise application form
- supporting plans/reports etc., and
- apply for Exemption Certificate at least 30 days before tipping commences.

❑ Is a water discharge consent required? If yes
- a separate consent is required for each discharge
- completion of application form(s), and
- cheque for fees.

❑ Is a trade effluent consent required? If yes
- a separate consent is required for each discharge
- notification of sewerage undertaker, and
- cheque for fees.

❑ Is there adequate insurance, with appropriate pollution cover where necessary? If not
- consult with broker; and
- read policy-wordings with care.

❑ Are site-personnel adequately prepared to cope with an environmental crisis?
- consider possible scenarios, pollution events, protestor action etc.
- prepare emergency plan designed to cope with most eventualities
- ensure relevant staff are familiar with their roles, and
- consider whether additional insurance is required.

On-site checklist

☐ Have the potential hazards which may be posed by the site been assessed? If not
- conduct preliminary survey and
- make enquiries of relevant authorities.

☐ Has the location of any underground pipelines, cables or sewers been checked ?

☐ Has the proximity of watercourses been checked for both surface and ground water?

☐ Are there adequate protection measures in place to prevent water pollution? If not
- bunding and/or pumping where necessary, and
- security measures to prevent trespassers/vandalism.

☐ Are any hazardous substances known to be on-site?
- conduct risk assessment, and
- make provisions for safe storage and handling.

☐ Are employees adequately trained and equipped to deal with them?
- employee awareness campaign, and
- provision of protective equipment.

☐ Are there adequate procedures in place for management of waste?
- check conditions of WML if relevant, and
- establish appropriate handling procedures on site.

☐ Is it known how to comply with the Duty of Care?
- store and pack waste so as to prevent its escape
- decribe clearly its constituent parts
- deal only with authorised waste carriers
- provide accurate transfer notes relating to the waste, and
- ensure waste is ultimately disposed of correctly.

☐ Has consideration been given to minimising noise, smell and dust emissions from the site?
- consider prior consultation/discussion with local community
- consider application for s.61 consent, and
- check contractual/insurance position in the event of third-party claims.

Post-contract checklist

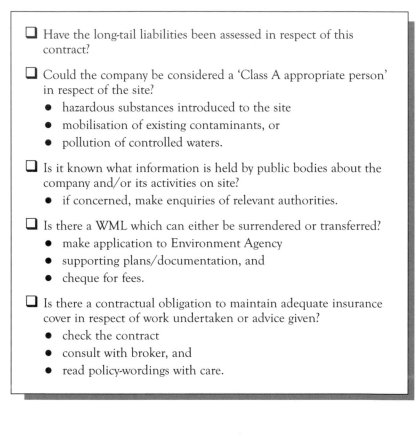

❑ Have the long-tail liabilities been assessed in respect of this contract?

❑ Could the company be considered a 'Class A appropriate person' in respect of the site?
- hazardous substances introduced to the site
- mobilisation of existing contaminants, or
- pollution of controlled waters.

❑ Is it known what information is held by public bodies about the company and/or its activities on site?
- if concerned, make enquiries of relevant authorities.

❑ Is there a WML which can either be surrendered or transferred?
- make application to Environment Agency
- supporting plans/documentation, and
- cheque for fees.

❑ Is there a contractual obligation to maintain adequate insurance cover in respect of work undertaken or advice given?
- check the contract
- consult with broker, and
- read policy-wordings with care.

Table of statutes
and European Council directives

STATUTES

EUROPEAN COUNCIL DIRECTIVES

Table of statutory instruments

Management of Health and Safety at Work Regulations 1999 (SI 1999/3242), 131

Personal Protective Equipment at Work Regulations 1992 (SI 1992/2966), 105-106
Planning (Hazardous Substances) Regulations 1992 (SI 1992/656), 35
Pollution Prevention and Control (England and Wales) Regulations 2000 (SI 2000/1973), 36, 73

Special Waste Regulations 1996 (SI 1996/972), 65-66
Statutory Nuisance (Appeals) Regulations 1995, 109

Town and Country Planning (Applications) Regulations 1988 (SI 1998/1812), 26
Town and Country Planning (Environmental Impact Assessment) (England and Wales) Regulations 1999 (SI 1999/293), 39-46
Town and Country Planning (Fees for Applications and Deemed Applications) Regulations 1989 (SI 1989/193), 26
Town and Country Planning (General Permitted Development) Order 1995 (SI 1995/418), 25

Waste Management Licensing Regulations 1994 (SI 1994/1056), 68, 70

Table of cases

157

Inter-Environnement Wallonie v. Regione Wallonie (Case C-129/96) [1998]
   Env LR 625, 64-65

Jones v. Llanrwst UDC [1911] All ER 922, 16

Kent CC v. Queensborough Rolling Mill Co. Ltd [1990] JEL 257, 63

McDonald v. Associated Fuels [1954] 3 DLR 713, 16
Mayer Parry Recycling Ltd v. Environment Agency [1999] Env LR 489, 63,
   64
Meston Technical Services Ltd and Wright v. Warwickshire County Council
   [1995] Env LR D36, 63

NRA v. Biffa [1996] Env L R 227, 89

Pwllbach Colliery v. Woodman [1915] AC 634, 14

R. v. CPC (UK) Ltd [1994] *The Times* 4 August, 4
R. v. Imran and Hussein [1997] Crim LR 754, 138
Rylands v. Fletcher [1868] LR 3 HL 330, 12-13, 47

Sherras v. De Rutzen [1895] 1 QB 918 at 922, 4

Video London Sound Studios v. Asticus (GMS) and Keltbray Demolition Ltd
   [2001] PLC 12 (4) p.66, 11

Woodhouse v. Walsall MBC [1994] Env LR 30, 6

Bibliography

Bell, S. and McGillivray, D., *Ball and Bell on Environmental Law – The Law and Policy Relating to the Protection of the Environment*, 5th Edition, Blackstone Press Limited, London, 2000

Circular 21/87: *Development of Contaminated Land* (DoE 1987)

Circular 17/89: *Landfill Sites – Development Control* (DoE 1989)

Circular 11/91: *Controlled Waste – Registration of Carriers and Seizure of Vehicles* (DoE 1991)

Circular 11/92: *Planning Controls for Hazardous Substances* (DoE 1992)

Circular 4/93: *Control of Injurious Substances* (DoE 1993)

Circular 8/93: *Unreasonable Behaviour* (DoE 1993)

Circular 11/94: *Waste Management Licensing* (DoE 1994)

Circular 10/95: *Planning Controls over Demolition* (DoE 1995)

Circular 11/95: *The Use of Conditions in Planning Permissions* (DoE 1995)

Circular 6/96: *Special Waste* (DoE 1996)

Circular 9/97: *Noise and Statutory Nuisance* (DoE 1997)

Circular 2/99: *Environmental Impact Assessment* (DETR 1999)

Circular 2/2000: *Contaminated Land* (DETR 2000)

Circular 8/2000: *Town and Country Planning (Residential Development on Greenfield Land) (England) Direction 2000* (DETR 2000)

Commission Decision on a List of Wastes (94/3/EC)

Draft Statutory Guidance on Contaminated Land – 2 Volumes (DoE 1996)

Consolidated List of National Planning Policy (DTLR, www.dtlr.gov.uk)

Tromans, Stephen and Turrall-Clarke, Robert, *Contaminated Land – The New Regime*, Sweet and Maxwell, London, 2000

Environment Agency Enforcement Policy Statement (Environment Agency 1996)

Environment Agency Enforcement and Prosecution Policy (Environment Agency 1998)

Environment Agency Functional Guidelines (Environment Agency 2001)

Environment Agency: Management Statement (DoE 1996)

Environment Agency and Sustainable Development (DoE 1996)

Fifth Environmental Action Programme – Towards Sustainability (COM (92) 23)

Fink, S. *'Masons' Guide: Health and Safety Law for the Construction Industry'* (1997) Thomas Telford: London

Framework for Contaminated Land: Paying for our Past (DoE 1994)

Guide to Risk Assessment and Risk Management for Environmental Protection (DoE 1995)

Guidelines for Baseline Ecological Assessment (Institute of Environmental Management and Assessment, www.iema.net)

Guidelines for Environmental Assessment of Road Traffic (Institute of Environmental Management and Assessment, www.iema.net)

ICE *Conditions of Contract*, 7th edition, Thomas Telford, London, 1999

Information Note 1/97 on *Reclamation of Contaminated Land* (HM Customs and Excise)

List of wastes pursuant to Article 1(a) of Directive 75/442/EEC on waste and Article (4) of Directive 91/689/EEC on hazardous waste. ('European Waste Catalogue' Commission Decision 2000/532/EC 315/00)

PPG 1 – *General Policy and Principles* (DoE 1997)

PPG 3 – *Housing* (DETR 2000)

PPG 10 – *Planning and Waste Management* (DETR 1999)

PPG 11 – *Regional Planning* (DETR 2000)

PPG 14 – *Development on Unstable Land* (DoE 1990)

PPG 23 – *Planning and Pollution Control* (DoE 1994)

Prevention and Reduction of Environmental Pollution by Asbestos Direction 1996 (Environment Agency 1996)

Screening, Scoping and ES Review under the 1999 Environmental Impact Assessment Regulations, Working Paper 184 (2000) (Oxford Brookes University Impact Assessment Unit)

Town and Country Planning (Demolition – Description of Buildings) Direction 1995 (DoE 1995)

Treasury Taskforce *Guidance on the Standardisation of PFI Controls*
Waste Management Licensing (Fees and Charges) Scheme (Environment Agency 1997)
Waste Management: *The Duty of Care: A Code of Practice* (DoE 1996)
Waste Management Paper No. 4 – *Licensing of Waste Management Facilities* (DoE 1994)

USEFUL WEBSITES
Aberystwyth University EIA Unit – *www.aber.ac.uk*
Chartered Institute of Water and Environmental Management – *www.ciwem.org.uk*
Civil Engineering Contractors Association – *www.ceca.co.uk*
Construction Best Practice Programme – *www.cbpp.org.uk*
Construction Industry Board – *www.ciboard.org.uk*
Considerate Construction Scheme – *www.ccscheme.org.uk*
Construction Industry Research and Information Association – *www.ciria.org.uk/environment.htm*
Dept of the Environment, Food and Rural Affairs – *www.defra.gov.uk*
Dept for Transport, Local Government and the Regions – *www.dtlr.gov.uk*
Environment Agency – *www.environment-agency.gov.uk*
Envirowise – *www.envirowise.gov.uk*
Health and Safety Executive – *www.hse.gov.uk*
Institution of Civil Engineers – *www.icenet.org*
Institute of Environmental Assessment – *www.iema.net*
National Chemical Emergency Centre – *www.the-ncec.com*
Royal Institution of Chartered Surveyors – *www.rics.org.uk*

Index

definition, 130
DOs and DON'Ts, 146-147
enforcing authorities, 133-136
generalisations, 132-133
interviews, 136-139
legal obligation, 130
polluting incidents, 139-141
protesters, 141-145
regulatory powers, 133-136
summary, 146-147
crushing, 73
Customs and Excise, 82-84

D and O see Directors' and Officers'
  Indemnity
damages, 14
defences
  abatement notices, 110-111
  water pollution, 93
demolition, 25, 61, 111
Department of the Environment,
  33, 40, 50, 52, 53
development, 29-30, 33-34
Directive waste, 62-63
  definition, 61, 64
Directors' and Officers' Indemnity
  (D and O) insurance, 114, 120
discharge
  consents, 88-91
  controlled waters, 88-96
  definition, 89-90
disposal to sewers, 98-99
District Councils, 21
DOs and DON'Ts, 146-147
Drinking Water Inspectorate, 18
dust, 19
duty of care, waste management, 60,
  76-78, 79, 81

EAR see Employers' All Risks
EIA see Environmental Impact
  Assessments

EIL see Environmental Impairment
  Liability
EL see Employers' Liability
employees, 104-106, 114
Employers' All Risks (EAR)
  insurance, 113, 117
Employers' Liability (EL) insurance,
  114
enforcement
  authorities, 133-136, 146
  development controls, 33-34
  statutory nuisance, 108-110
Enforcement and Prosecution
  Policy, 17, 92, 138
Environment Agency, 17-19
  Enforcement and Prosecution
    Policy, 138
  registration, 73
  waste management, 66, 73
  water pollution, 96-97
Environmental Impact Assessments
  (EIA), 21, 39-46
  practice, 40-46
  requirement, 40-41
Environmental Impairment Liability
  (EIL), 121-123
environmental management systems,
  131
Environmental Statements, 39-40,
  42-46
  preparation, 44-45
  submission, 45-46
European Waste Catalogue, 61, 63
exemptions, 70-74, 82-84, 88-89
expert advice, 141

fines, 34, 53, 67, 79, 92, 99, 111
  see also costs
fit and proper persons, 68, 69
Food and Rural Affairs, Secretary of
  State for, 22
Formal Cautions, 7-8

fumes, 19
Functional Guidelines, 17, 18, 92, 138
  see also Common Incident Classification Scheme

grinding, 73
grit, 19
guides, 106

hazardous substances, 104
health and safety, 2, 6, 102, 106, 131
Health and Safety Commission, 105
Her Majesty's Inspectorate of Pollution (HMIP), 17
highway planning, 32
HMIP *see* Her Majesty's Inspectorate of Pollution
human rights, 145

imprisonment, 101
incident reporting, 133-134
insurance, 113-127
  claims-made basis, 123
  environmental risks, 114-120
  exclusions, 117
  traditional policies, 114-120
Integrated Pollution Control (IPC), 27, 35-37
Integrated Pollution Prevention and Control (IPPC) system, 18-20, 27, 35-37, 55
interviews under caution, 136-139
investment, 113-127
IPC *see* Integrated Pollution Control
IPPC *see* Integrated Pollution Prevention and Control system

knowingly permit events, 93-96

land *see* contaminated land
landfill taxes, 53, 59, 80-84

Custom and Excise, 82-84
  exemptions, 82-84
  price increases, 80, 81
  regime, 80-81
lender liability, 113, 123-127
liability
  backstop, 126
  civil, 8-16
  contaminated land, 54-57
  contracts, 9-10
  criminal, 4-8
  lenders, 113, 123-127
  personal, 6-7
  tort, 10-16
  for what, 3-16
  who is liable, 3-16
listed buildings, 25-26
local authorities, 19-22, 50-51

major accident reporting, 133
management
  water resources, 17
  see also crisis management; waste management
mortgages, 124-127

National Rivers Authority (NRA), 17
negligence, tort, 13-16
noise, 107-108, 111-112
non-compliance, 110-111
NRA *see* National Rivers Authority
nuclear industry, 14-15, 131, 133
nuisance, 11-13, 101
  noise, 107-108, 111-112
  see also statutory nuisance

occupiers, 68, 103
offences, 67, 78-79, 91-94, 106-112, 144
Office of Water Services (OFWAT), 99
on-site checklist, 151-152